P9-DMK-109

*T*his book
belongs to

Debbie Meritt

*...a woman with a
high calling from God.*

A Woman's High Calling

Elizabeth George

HARVEST HOUSE PUBLISHERS
Eugene, Oregon 97402

Unless otherwise indicated, all Scripture quotations are taken from the New King James Version, Copyright © 1979, 1980, 1982 by Thomas Nelson, Inc., Publishers. Used by permission. All rights reserved.

Verses marked NASB are taken from the New American Standard Bible, © 1960, 1962, 1963, 1968, 1971, 1972, 1973, 1975, 1977 by The Lockman Foundation. Used by permission.

Verses marked KJV are taken from the King James Version of the Bible.

Verses marked RSV are taken from the Revised Standard Version of the Bible, Copyright © 1946, 1952, 1971 by the Division of Christian Education of the National Council of the Churches of Christ in the U.S.A. Used by permission.

Cover by Terry Dugan Design, Minneapolis, Minnesota

~ Acknowledgments

As always, thank you to my dear husband, Jim George, M.Div., Th.M., for your able assistance, guidance, suggestions, and loving encouragement on this project.

A WOMAN'S HIGH CALLING
Copyright © 2001 By Elizabeth George
Published by Harvest House Publishers
Eugene, Oregon 97402

Library of Congress Cataloging-in-Publication Data

George, Elizabeth, 1944-
    A woman's high calling / Elizabeth George.
        p. cm.
    ISBN 0-7369-0327-5
        1. Christian women—Religious life. I. Title.

BV4527 .G465 2001
248.8′43—dc21   2001024086

All rights reserved. No part of this publication may be reproduced, stored in a retrieval system, or transmitted in any form or by any means—electronic, mechanical, digital, photocopy, recording, or any other—except for brief quotations in printed reviews, without the prior permission of the publisher.

Printed in the United States of America.

01 02 03 04 05 06 07 08 09 10 / BP-KB / 10 9 8 7 6 5 4 3

Contents

A companion study guide,
*A Woman's High Calling Growth
and Study Guide,* is available.

A Prayer for Godly Living

"Lord, help me to be a godly woman!"

I was hearing it again. It was Wednesday night, Bible study night. And scattered throughout the downstairs of our home were small groups of college students praying. It was my practice each week to slip in and out of the women's groups to hear their hearts at prayer, to sort of keep my finger on their spiritual pulses. And, sure enough, time after time, I'd hear this heartfelt prayer from woman after woman: "Lord, help me to be a godly woman!"

And always, upon hearing those young women's plea, my mind would wander back to my own heartfelt prayers and impassioned pleas to God over the decades as I, too, had prayed, "Lord, help me to be a godly woman!" Yes, I had prayed often—daily!...and still do...that God would please help *me* to be a godly woman! Indeed, my heart yearns to approach that high calling every day!

But I've also learned a large lesson about that plea—it's *vague*. Yes, it's a most worthy prayer...but it is vague. Therefore over the years I've begun not only to pray to *be* a godly woman but also to ask, "What does a godly woman *do?* How does she *act?* What is it about her that *marks* her out as a godly woman?"

With these questions to direct me, I set out several decades ago to find out what it means to be a godly woman. And that, dear reader, is what this book is all about. It's about what I call "the pink passages" in the Bible, which spell out God's high calling for us as His women. You see, I always read my Bible with a pink marker in hand. Then, when I hit a passage that has to do with women—the women of the Bible, the role of women in the Bible, the qualities (good and bad) that God mentions regarding women—I highlight it, knowing that I've found some verses that I want to dig into in my quest to define the godly woman.

Well, the time has come to put some of the findings from these "diggings" down on paper—specifically, from Titus 2:3-5. I have to admit up front that this passage of Scripture and this undertaking hasn't been easy. In fact, I've tried many times to satisfactorily teach these truths and to write this book. No, it hasn't been easy to study and communicate God's high callings to us as His women. Why? Because many of the words used to describe a godly woman's traits are found only once in the Bible. And harder than the *study* of these qualities and characteristics has been the *application* of them! You see, once you've seen and handled and tasted the elements of our high calling, there's no doubt you have to *do* something with them! They invite you to pursue God's high calling...or to refuse it. To seek it...or to shirk it.

So, do you want to grow in knowledge and in grace? Do you want to learn more about being "a godly woman"? Do you want to develop a good set of worthwhile lifetime goals? Do you want to move toward fulfilling a life-long dream of becoming God's kind of woman?

Then utter an earnest prayer, and let's look, listen, and learn from the Lord. Let's find out more about God's essentials for women and prayerfully set some goals that will help to move us in the right direction—His direction, the direction of His high and upward calling...

...a calling to godly living.

Essential 1

"the older women [are to] be
reverent in behavior"
—TITUS 2:3

"How are we to live our lives as women with a
high calling? Our calling is to godly behavior, to
sacred behavior, to holy behavior. Our conduct
must complement our high calling in Christ."

"Can you fathom any higher calling than
godliness? Any more important essential for
godly living? Can you imagine any more
wonderful way to spend your life and your time
and your days and your moments than to spend
them in the Lord, immersed in Him, looking to
Him, desiring Him and the riches (and the
richness!) of His grace above all that this poor
world offers? You and I are above all others most
blessed to possess such a glorious calling!"

*C*hapter One

A Woman's High Calling to Godliness

*W*hat a treat I savored this past spring when I traveled with my husband Jim to England to attend our church's European missions conference! I had heard about the quaintness and the "oldeness" of England before, but now I had a God-given opportunity to taste it for myself.

One particular day turned out to be life-changing for me. You see, our host arranged an outing for our group to the legendary Canterbury Cathedral in Kent, England. The area of Kent has a rich Christian history, dating back to the days of Saint Augustine (A.D. 597), and the Canterbury Cathedral there is heralded as one of the finest ecclesiastical structures in England. I've never seen anything so magnificent!

Anyway, while Jim and I were walking through the 80-foot-high stone porticos of the cathedral and sitting in its centuries-old pews in order to take in the lofty archways, towering columns, and ornate ceilings, we became quietly aware of the clergy who tended to the church and the people who worshiped there. They moved about silently—so silently that we were never distracted. They moved reverently—never for a second forgetting that they were in a place of worship. They spoke little, if at all, and always in quiet tones. One could almost sense their awareness that they were in the presence of God.

The already ethereal ambiance was further heightened by the sounds of a women's choir in rehearsal. Their voices and the strains of their hymns literally soared upward (and without the aid of a man-made audio system!) to the heights of the nave and then drifted down again, filling the 522-foot length of the cathedral with an inescapable sweetness. The women, singing without accompaniment as they practiced for the Evensong Service to be held later that day, were nowhere in sight. In fact, we had to go searching for them. Peering through an iron gate, we caught a mere glimpse of them, all dressed alike in black skirts and white blouses, standing behind the aged wooden railings that marked out the choir loft, singing in unison to the Lord, quite oblivious to the many who sought to get a peek at them.

Everything about our visit to the Canterbury Cathedral was spiritually uplifting! Why? Well, certainly the majestic architecture contributed to our experience. But, more than the place, the *people* who served and worshiped with reverence there inspired the same in us. Suddenly we found ourselves whispering. Why? They were quiet...therefore we were quiet. Without our noticing, our breakneck tourist pace slowed to a stroll. Why? Because they were moving silently, reverently, worshipfully (if there is such a word)...therefore we did, too. One couldn't help but pray in such a place. Again, why? Because the church attendants and choir seemed to be absorbed in worship and in the God they served...therefore we were, too.

All this reminded both Jim and me that we were not in a museum or a well-preserved architectural model. No. As I said, we were in a place of worship. And somehow, the reverential behavior of others brought to us a fresh awareness of God's presence. We'll never forget that wonderful spring afternoon in England!

God's High Calling to Godliness

Now, are you wondering how touring a church in beautiful England relates to you and me and our high calling as women? Quite simply, that experience provided an opportunity to see and experience firsthand (and to share with you) the kind of conduct God has in mind for us as His women. As we step into our study of God's high calling we meet up, in Titus 2:3-5 (one of those "pink passages" in the Bible that deal with women), with God's calling to *godliness*. Obviously, *godliness* is one of the essentials for *godly* living. And it summons us to an all-consuming commitment to God and a pursuit meant to permeate every area of our life.

But I must warn you—there's no tiptoeing into our calling. There's no warming-up to the godly qualities that we'll be looking at in this book. And there's no apprenticeship. No, God doesn't ease us into His summons on our life. He instead commences His call right at the core, at the deepest (and highest!) level of our calling—and that is this first calling, a calling to Himself. Because what's inside our hearts affects our behavior, God asks that our relationship with Him be the catalyst that creates in us behavior befitting one who has a relationship with the living God. He wants our actions to be reverent, godly, worshipful, and holy, mirroring a heart that is reverent, godly, worshipful, and holy. He states, "the older women likewise, that they be reverent in their behavior" (verse 3), or as the King James Version so wonderfully conveys, "that they be in behavior as becometh holiness."

We find these words of scripture—Titus 2:3-5—in the short epistle the apostle Paul wrote to his helper, Titus, a trusted assistant sent to aid the church in Crete. Paul's letter to Titus addressed the issue of order in the church and the tasks and responsibilities of the different groups that make up a congregation—the pastor (verse 1), the older men (verse 2), the older women (verse 3), the younger women (verses 4-5), and the younger men (verse 6). And even though the call to this particular quality—*godliness*—is addressed to "the older women" in the body of Christ (verse 3), it wraps its arms around each and every woman...regardless of age. Why? Because it points first to our spirit of worship and calls us to be reverent in all our behavior (Titus 2:3).

As I said, it's a *high* calling!

Learning About Godliness

Do you remember my mentioning in my preface, "A Prayer for Godly Living," that many of the words that define our high calling are used only once in the Bible? Well, that's true of this first and foremost quality of holy and reverent behavior. In fact, it's a unique combination of two Greek words that is used only here in the New Testament.

- *The first word is reverent (hieroprepes)*—meaning sacred *(hieros)* and to be fitting *(prepo)*. In simple language, it marks out what is fitting and appropriate and suited to sacred character. Put another way, it describes persons, actions, or things consecrated to God. Its many synonyms include sacred, reverent and reverend, along with holy.

- *The second word is behavior (katastema)*—having to do with the condition of something.

> Such synonyms as deportment and demeanor,
> indicating the external conduct (our behavior,
> manner, and carriage) as manifesting the inner
> life, help us understand.

When the ideas of these two words are put together, they mean *reverent in behavior*. You see, our *behavior* stems from a state of mind, from what's going on (or not going on!) in our inner life, and God desires that the behavior of His women be *reverent*, behavior mirroring an internal sacred character.

As one scholar explains, *reverent in behavior* means "consecrated as priestesses."[1] The idea is that we are to exhibit— physically and spiritually—in all of daily life, the demeanor of a temple priestess. Yes, priestlike defines the flavor of reverent behavior in that it is "befitting or becoming sacred persons."[2] There is to be about our lives a reverential spirit of consecration and dedication that is consistent with the fact of our spiritual priesthood.[3] As my pastor writes, this word reverent "has the root meaning of being priestlike and came to refer to that which is appropriate to holiness."[4]

Living Out Godliness

That's quite a start, isn't it? Words such as "consecrated," "holy," "sacred," and "worship" speak loudly of a heart and mind set on our thrice-holy God and the worship of Him. Such a one has to have a soul preoccupied with God, a soul immersed in a constant state of worship of God, a soul completely consecrated to God. Such a soul...and such resulting behavior...would then certainly point others to God! Think now of the clergy and the women's choir in the cathedral at Canterbury. As I tried to express, they modeled for me what reverent behavior looks like, how one who is in a constant state of worship acts, and the inspiring effect one who is consumed with the worship of the Lord has on others.

Beloved, this is how you and I are to live *our* lives as women with a high calling. You see, our calling is to godly behavior, to sacred behavior, to holy behavior. Our conduct must complement our high calling in Christ. It must match our calling to be engaged in sacred things, the things of the Lord. We are to walk through the minutes and the hours, the days and the decades, of our life as a priestess would walk through and serve in a temple. We must live our lives as if all of life were a sacred assembly. We must apply to all of daily life the reverent demeanor, the sacred conduct, and the holy behavior of a priestess in a temple. That, dear one, is our high calling from God, a calling to godliness.

Yes, it is quite a picture! And so our lives, too, are to be lived with a demeanor and behavior, a state and a condition, that fits a holy woman, a woman who is reverent in her behavior, a woman who goes about the business of worshiping the God she loves and serves—day in and day out. Our reverential, godly behavior should include the whole habit and composition or structure of mind and body, encompassing not only the movements of the body, but also the expression of the countenance, and what is said and what is left unsaid.[5]

Godliness Lived Out in Another

Are your thoughts reeling with images of priestesses and holy women? Well, it's always good to see such an awesome, otherworldly, hard-to-define quality like *godliness* lived out and fleshed out in other women. After all, as the saying instructs us, "One picture *is* worth a thousand words!" And when it comes to an older woman who was reverent and godly and holy in her behavior, you and I can thank the Lord for the woman in the Bible named Anna. Her story is found in Luke 2:36-38. In just three verses! But these three God-breathed verses brilliantly describe this holy woman who trusted in God (1 Peter 3:5) and show us a woman who was truly reverent in her behavior. Read them now.

> Now there was one, Anna, a prophetess, the daughter of Phanuel, of the tribe of Asher. She was of a great age, and had lived with a husband seven years from her virginity; and this woman was a widow of about eighty-four years, who did not depart from the temple, but served God with fastings and prayers night and day. And coming in that instant she gave thanks to the Lord, and spoke of Him to all those who looked for redemption in Jerusalem.

Luke's words paint a poignant picture of this dear woman. From him we learn that Anna was an "older woman." An 84-year-old woman ("of a great age," explains Luke), Anna was widowed after only seven years of marriage. And Anna shows us (quite literally!) what it's like to live in a constant state of worship. What does a woman do who loves the Lord and is a widow? Well, our Anna apparently devoted herself to the continual service of God and of His temple. She was a constant, devout worshiper—not a casual attender or observer.

- She lived her life *in the temple.* Anna's life, which could have been a long, sad, and lonely one, was instead filled with glorious service to God and was centered on the temple, the worship of God, and the people who exalted Him there. Indeed, it appears that she never left the temple, but lived there on the temple grounds, serving God night and day.

- She lived her life *in prayer and fasting.* Both prayer and fasting are personal disciplines—*quiet* disciplines—requiring commitment, dedication, self-control, and consecration to God. Anna devoted herself to these quiet disciplines and to a quiet, serious life of loving and worshiping God.

- She lived her life *in anticipation of the Savior.* Like Simeon, who loved God and waited for God to save His people (Luke 2:25), Anna also looked for the Christ...and was blessed to see the baby Jesus when He was brought into the temple for the first time, to praise God for Him, and to speak of Jesus to all who entered the temple.

When I think of my own busy life and the multiple roles I must live out each day (and I know I'm not alone in this!), I have to admit I sometimes yearn for a quiet life...like Anna's, a life filled with quietly and constantly and literally worshiping our God. Imagine! One role—to love the Lord your God with all your heart, soul, mind, and strength. In one place—the house of the Lord. And for all the days of your life! Anna, our model for reverent and holy behavior, was allowed, through the circumstances of her life, to fulfill (in fact!) the desire every one of God's people possesses, the desire the psalmist David dreamed of when he wrote, "One thing I have desired of the LORD, that will I seek: That I may dwell in the house of the LORD all the days of my life, to behold the beauty of the LORD, and to inquire in His temple" (Psalm 27:4).

Following Our Calling to Godliness

But, while Anna literally and *physically* dwelt in the house of the Lord and walked in His temple and served Him there, you and I can (and are called to) do the same *spiritually.* How?

✓ *Pray*—Prayer will most definitely affect our behavior! The act of prayer brings our soul into direct contact with the God we worship and love, so it stands to reason that the more we pray, the more we're aware of the presence of the Lord, and the more we reflect His beauty and godliness to others.

Here's a thought—my friend Judy visited an antique shop where she found a treasure the owner referred to as "a prayer clock." This unique timepiece chimed on every hour. That's nothing unusual. But her prayer clock also chimed at five minutes *after* every hour! Its first sound was a call to prayer and its second sound was the signal that prayertime was over. What a refreshing idea! Perhaps you can pause every hour for some holy minutes of prayer.

✓ *Purpose*—to be more aware of God's presence.

> Worship is an inward reverence,
> the bowing down of the soul in the presence
> of God,...a solemn consciousness of the Divine,
> a secret communion with the unseen.[6]

As I said before, we *know* God is always present, indeed omnipresent. But the woman who lives her life in a constant state of worship and cultivates the habit of holiness lives her day-in, day-out life with a keen awareness of the very presence of God! So purpose to develop a solemn consciousness of the Divine and to deliberately bow down your soul in His presence. That awareness and God's enablement will cause you to be reverent in behavior.

✓ *Praise the Lord*—Are you unsure of exactly how to praise the Lord? Or is life so sorrowful...or frantic...or complex...that it's difficult to praise Him? Why not follow the advice of another saint who recommended reading one Psalm out loud every day? Then allow the Psalm to feed your heart so that your lips gush with praise and worship to the Lord. As he explains,

> You are to consider this [reading] of a psalm as a necessary beginning of your devotion, something that is to awaken all that is good and holy within you, that is to call your spirits to their proper duty, to set you in your best posture towards heaven, and tune all the powers of your soul to worship and adoration. For there is nothing that so clears a way for your prayers, nothing that so disperses dullness of heart, nothing that so purifies the soul from poor and careless passions, nothing that so opens heaven, or carries your heart so near to it, as these songs of praise.[7]

✓ *And praise Him some more!*—Perhaps the theme song of women who are (and seek to be) in a constant state of worship and live (and seek to live) their lives in reverent and holy behavior might be this:

> Fill thou my life, O Lord my God,
> In every part with praise,
> That my whole being may proclaim
> Thy being and thy ways.
> Not for the lip of praise alone,
> Nor e'en the praising heart,
> I ask, but for a life made up
> Of praise in every part.[8]

✓ *Pick*—a point for meditation. Thinking on a particular attribute of God, some act or teaching of Jesus, a promise from God's Word, or some calling from Scripture will tune your heart to the Lord. As you carry thoughts like these into your day's demands, your soul will shine and you will truly exhibit the presence of the Lord and the powerful effect of His Word on your life.

✓ *Prize*—your high calling to reverent behavior. It's a calling to bask in the presence of the Lord! The consecrated, set-apart life of holiness is true bliss—not old-fashioned or undesirable. It doesn't mean that you can't laugh. Nor does it mean you're ungodly if you joke with your children! And it doesn't mean that you should turn into a sanctimonious, stiff, and prudish woman, wife, mother, or co-worker. No. But it *does* mean that you weed out antics, humor, sarcasm, stunts, and speech that are irreverent, and any other behaviors that have no place in the life of a woman who is called to be in continual fellowship with God. Own your high calling! Prize it! Revel in it! And excel in it!

✓ *Plan*—to act in ways that attract attention to the Lord rather than to yourself. Make it your goal to behave (by God's grace!) in such a way that others are spiritually influenced and drawn into worship rather than distracted from it. May your life and the choices you make tell others of your wonderful God as you walk through life in a constant state of worship, as a priestess unto Him.

✓ *Ponder*—your behavior and your choices, for by them you tell on yourself. This poem, although a little old and dated, definitely gets the point across!

You Tell on Yourself

You tell on yourself by the friends you seek,
By the very manner in which you speak,
By the way you employ your leisure time,
By the use you make of dollar and dime.

You tell what you are by the things you wear,
By the spirit in which you burdens bear,
By the kind of things at which you laugh,
By the records you play on the phonograph,

You tell what you are by the way you walk,
By the things of which you delight to talk,
By the manner in which you bear defeat,
By so simple a thing as how you eat.

By the books you choose from the
    well-filled shelf:
In these ways and more, you tell on yourself.[9]

Looking Upward

How is your high calling looking so far, dear friend? Here it is (or at least the first and foremost element of it): a calling to worship God in spirit and truth, to worship Him in the beauty of holiness. It's glorious! It's divine! It is a truly magnificent calling—there's no doubt about it. But, oh, to think of actually *answering* God's calling for godliness and godly behavior in our lives! (Can't you just taste it?!) Just think of the consummate joy God graces our lives with when we seek to be consumed with Him, to love Him supremely, to follow Him fully, to fill our hearts and minds, souls and spirits with His Holy Word and with holy thoughts of Him.

Can you fathom any higher calling? Any more important essential for godly living? Can you imagine any more wonderful way to spend your life and your time and your days and your moments than to spend them *in* the Lord, *immersed* in Him, *looking* to Him, *desiring* Him and the riches (and the rich*ness!*) of His grace above and beyond all that this poor world offers? You and I, my precious sister, are above all others most blessed to possess such a glorious calling!

So, won't you please look to Him now? Turn your gaze upward, toward your high calling. It's a fact that the first step toward any noble goal is to desire it. And what a truly "godly" goal it is to follow God's will for your life and to set your affections on truly desiring to become this woman the Bible exalts so highly and points us to—a woman whose whole soul is absorbed in worshiping Him.

Essential 1

"the older women [are to] be
reverent in behavior"
—TITUS 2:3

"It is as your soul is constantly dwelling on the
God you love and serve and on His awesome,
holy presence that your behavior will
show forth your reverence for Him and
evoke the same in others."

"Your state of worship causes others to think
of God, too, and will move them to worship right
along with you. In other words, they
will not be able to be in your presence
without thinking about God."

Chapter Two

Godliness—An Essential for Godly Living

Most women are familiar with homemaking guru Martha Stewart's now-famous saying, "It's a good thing." Well, when it comes to good things, it's a good thing to take God's standards and make them our own. It's a good thing to seize what we learn from God's Word and set about to make it true of our life.

And that, dear one, is what these practical chapters subtitled "An Essential for Godly Living" will be all about— about incorporating God's will and God's ways and God's Word into our own lives. Throughout this book we want to, first of all, learn all that we can about exactly what God wants from and for us as His women. That's what I hope the ten essential qualities addressed in this book will bring to each of us. And, after we've gained an understanding of His Word (as we did in the previous chapter concerning God's high calling to *godliness*), we most definitely want to heed His calling and look to the Lord for His help...and then dive in to do our part to make His ways our ways, to answer His calling in very practical ways. We want to initiate—and follow!—a course of action that will put us on the path of God's will and (hopefully and prayerfully!) help us to make some progress down that path.

So with this practical focus in mind, let's begin our journey toward one of God's good things for us as women— the goal of *godliness*. Let's see how we can cultivate conduct and nurture behavior that speaks well of God.

Meet Mary Jane

I can never think about God's high calling on our life to behave like women who are in a constant state of worship without thinking of Mary Jane. This summons from God to sacred behavior sounds so impossible, so "out there," so other-worldly. In today's flashy, self-absorbed society, it's unfathomable, foreign, and does not compute! I admit I struggled when I first read these verses in the tiny book of Titus. And yet I now know exactly what this high calling to godliness means because I know Mary Jane.

Mary Jane is the pianist at my church, and I've been privileged to not only listen to Mary Jane play the piano for 27 years, but also to watch her life. You see, Mary Jane's "place" during our worship services is on the platform. It's a large platform, and very public—right *up there* in front of thousands of worshipers and right *out there* under blazing lights. And there Mary Jane sits. That's her place.

And yet I have to tell you that I almost don't even notice Mary Jane. (And, as you'll soon see, that's a compliment to her!) Why? Because Mary Jane is serving the Lord. She's not performing. Just like Anna in Luke 2, Mary Jane is herself worshiping the Lord. She is "performing" her service unto the Lord. And she's in His presence. She knows that, and somehow we in the congregation know that too. As we learned in the last chapter from one of our definitions of godliness, her behavior is sacred because her role is sacred and her worship is sacred.

For years (because I'd never met her) I never heard Mary Jane say a word. And there are a few other *nevers* to go along with that one. In 27 years of seeing her on the platform, I've never seen her wave or gesture or wink or make a face at anyone. I've never seen her chew gum or yawn. I've never seen her primp or fuss over her clothes, hair, or hands. I've never seen her wear anything inappropriate or immodest. I've never seen her make a "grand" entrance, although she ascends and descends the steps on the worship platform every week. She even moves from her piano bench to a nearby chair and back...yet, because of her own state and because of the solemnness of the occasion (it's our worship service), I'm never aware that she's even moved.

And then one day I met Mary Jane. I now know her fairly well. And guess what? Everything about her private life fits with the image I see in public. She's a lady. She's somewhat quiet. She's gracious. She's concerned about others. She's confident in a good way, in the Lord, and in the roles He has given her at home and at church and with the little ones she teaches at school. Of course she's fun and fun to be with, but there's a quiet seriousness about her, a settled seriousness about who she is (she's a child of God) and what she does with her life (she serves Him in everything she does).

I thank God regularly (and certainly, every Sunday!) for Mary Jane. In her He has given me a living, flesh-and-blood woman who shows me the way (many ways, in fact) to answer God's high calling to godliness, and to behavior and conduct that honors Him and represents Him well. She lives out for me the wonderful description and definition of godly behavior we looked at in the prior chapter: "Our reverential,

godly behavior should include the whole habit and composition or structure of mind and body, encompassing not only
the movements of the body, but also the expression of the
countenance, and what is said and what is left unsaid."[1]

With this summary of godliness in mind, I want us to
examine several of these elements. In this chapter I want us
to look carefully at *the mind* and *the mouth*.

The Meditations of the Mind

Your mind matters. In fact, it's crucial! For, as a man thinks
in his heart, so is he (see Proverbs 23:7). The New Testament, too, exhorts us to think on what is true, noble, just,
pure, lovely, good, virtuous, and praiseworthy (Philippians
4:8). Why? Because what we're thinking about and dwelling
upon and entertaining in our mind will ultimately show up
in our behavior.

So then, how can we exhibit the godly, reverent behavior
that Titus 2:3 suggests? One answer is obvious: We are to
think, as Paul said, "on these things"—the things that are
true, noble, just, pure, lovely, good, virtuous, and praiseworthy.

As a new Christian, I needed lots of Divine help! to begin
down the path of training my thoughts to turn heavenward
instead of focusing on the things of this world. It's still a
struggle to set my mind and affections on things above, not
on things on the earth. And, I might add, it's still a goal that
requires a willful decision and God's assistance each and
every day! But here are some things I seek to do that help
me in this area of godliness and godly thinking. I offer them
with a prayer that they might be of help to you, too.

- *Make a decision each day to seek to dwell on the
  Lord.* By this I mean turning my thoughts
  upward. I mean willfully thinking on God, on His

attributes, on portions of His Holy Word. I mean willfully contemplating what I read in my morning devotions all throughout the day. I mean willfully reflecting on verses I've memorized from the Bible, meditating and ruminating on them. I mean willfully choosing to think about the Lord instead of the news, instead of what someone said about someone else, instead of the lyrics to some song blaring out on the audio system in a store. And notice the word *willfully*. These are decisions and choices I try to remember to make as I walk through the days. It's like the age-old hymn urges, "*Turn* Your Eyes Upon Jesus"[2] (emphasis added).

- *Make sure your thoughts meet the guidelines of Philippians 4:8.* This is the scripture I referred to above that tells us to think on what is true, noble, just, pure, lovely, good, virtuous, and praise-worthy. Desiring to follow these criteria, I wondered, "What in the world could possibly meet these high standards?!" Well, a sure way to fulfill this divine ideal is dwelling on God, His Word, and His Son. So I recommend entertaining noble, lovely, good, etc., thoughts that center on the Godhead. Reflecting on such a virtuous subject as the God of the universe is sure to have a "godly" effect on our conduct!

- *Master the great hymns of the faith.* When our daughters were in grade school, we set a goal as a family to learn one hymn each month. I'm glad you didn't have to hear our attempts as a group to sing them without a piano or keyboard!

  But, while we may have sounded pretty awful, the music that was going into our hearts was precious! We each found ourselves humming our hymns all day long. They were contagious! We would even burst out singing these anthems while getting ready for work and school, while making the beds and the sack lunches, while riding in the car. These lofty, worshipful, sacred songs freely bubbled up from the recesses of mind and heart to lift us earthbound pilgrims heavenward. But...we had to put them into our souls in the first place!

- *Memorize scripture.* "Received July 15, 1980." These are the words written in pencil in the front of the textbook for my course titled *Memorize the Word.*[3] That's the date the book arrived in my mailbox. The next entry I wrote in the flyleaf of that book reads, "Begun July 16, 1980." And finally, over half a year later (actually almost eight months later!), I penned, "Finished March 5, 1981—PTL!" Why did I enroll in such a course to start with? Because I had tried...and tried...and *tried*...to memorize some of the many wonderful verses from the Bible that are packed with truth and meant so much to me...but with sure failure.

  But, with the Lord's help and this well-designed course from The Moody Bible Institute and eight months of diligent effort, I *finally* put the discipline of memorizing scripture into place in my Christian life! It's been life changing! I can now dip into my reservoir of memorized verses at any moment and lift them out of my heart to enjoy and use over and over again. God's Word in our hearts definitely helps us to think about Him. And, as I've said before, thoughts of Him never fail to transform our conduct!

- *Mark out certain times each day for praising God.* I love the psalmist's declaration to God in Psalm 119:164, "Seven times a day I praise You." Most scholars agree that the writer didn't mean seven literal times, but that by stating "seven" times, he was saying that he praised God *many* times or constantly, as continually and wholeheartedly as he could, throughout each day. But you can begin with seven. Why, that's as simple as praising Him when you say "grace" three times a day with your meals, once when you get up and once when you go to bed. Then surely you can fit in two more times each day!

  However, I did hear a woman speaker at our church share that she made it a point to think about the Lord and to praise Him each time she passed through the doorway to her kitchen. How many times a day would a woman pass through the doorway to her kitchen?! I can't even imagine! (Somehow, it's the most-visited room in any house!) But, try counting for yourself tomorrow. And better than counting, recount some wondrous fact about your God each time *you* pass through *your* kitchen doorway!

  > Sing praise to God who reigns above,
  > The God of all creation,
  > The God of power, the God of love,
  > The God of our salvation.[4]

As I said earlier, dear one, your mind matters. May this prayer of David's be yours—"Let the words of my mouth and *the meditation of my heart* be acceptable in your sight, O LORD....(Psalm 19:14, emphasis added).

Speaking of the mouth, God gives us guidelines for it!

Guidelines for the Mouth

Suppose you were in the presence of a woman who was thinking about God and enjoying sweet communion with Him as her thoughts ascended to His throne in prayer, who was continually absorbed in some portion of God's Holy Word, who was perhaps humming a hymn of praise to God. If you began to talk to one another, what do you imagine would come out of her mouth?

I think you can safely answer something like this: You would hear words of blessing, words filled with graciousness and sweetness from such a woman. Tumbling forth from her lips would be soothing, healing words of comfort or uplifting encouragement, whichever was appropriate. Certainly you would witness words of mercy, concern, and compassion.

And, so, you would find her to be like the woman of Proverbs 31:26—"She opens her mouth with wisdom and on her tongue is the law of kindness." Our description would not be complete without adding such adjectives as courteous, respectful, and honoring. Words of godly instruction (as we'll soon see when we get to God's fourth essential calling and goal for us—that we be teachers of good things) would also be the product of such a lady. And surely her communications would be pure and good (yet another two of God's words for us which we'll also cover in this book). Right away I thought of several examples of such women in the Bible and their utterances. We can learn important lessons from these women and their words. And, more than that, we can witness the effect of the mind and its musings on the mouth.

- *Anna*, as we learned in the previous chapter, was busy living out her life serving God with fastings and prayers when Mary and Joseph arrived with the newborn Jesus. We shouldn't be surprised that she gave thanks to the Lord and spoke of Him to anyone who would listen (Luke 2:36-38).

- *Elizabeth*, too, in Luke 1:41-42, was filled with the Holy Spirit and spoke forth praise and blessing when Mary, who was carrying the Savior in her womb, entered her house.

- *Mary*, in turn (also in Luke 1:46-55), broke forth in a song of pure praise called "Mary's Magnificat." Filled with Old Testament references and quotations, it reveals that Mary's heart and mind too were filled to overflowing with God's Word, indeed echoing the heartfelt prayers of Hannah, yet another godly woman (see 1 Samuel 1:1–2:10).

Contrast these models of godly thoughts leading to godly words with what we so often hear instead—murmuring and complaining. Gossip and slander. Vicious anger and bitter poison. Even hatred. The spewing of loud, boisterous, obnoxious utterances. Steaming words of argument. Or, another category that I've labeled "bathroom talk." Oh, to be like Anna, Elizabeth, and Mary instead! To be women who are aware of the Lord, who are worshiping the Lord, who have their thoughts set on the Lord, who then speak forth words that indicate the reality of a woman living out her high calling to godliness!

So now you (and I) must ask the hard question: What usually comes out of *my mouth?* Your answer is important, because, as someone has well observed,

A Christian is
a mind through which Christ thinks
a voice through which Christ speaks
a heart through which Christ loves
a hand through which Christ helps.[5]

As I said earlier, coming to grips with the fact that godliness was one of God's goals for my life as one of His women caused a great struggle in me. First I had to struggle to get to the bottom of (or at least go a little deeper into!) the meaning of godliness itself. Then, because I came to Christ out of the women's liberation movement, I had to struggle with whether or not I even *liked* the quality! (I thank God that I didn't have to struggle to find the quality lived out because He gave me Mary Jane and other women like her!) And I also had to struggle with the great *how*—*how* does one go about living out this essential calling?

Well, my dear reading friend, in addition to attempting to regularly practice what I've just outlined above regarding my mind, I also set about asking God for His help with my mouth so that my life *and my lips* might exemplify Christ. As the saying goes, "Faith makes a woman a Christian, but her life proves she is a Christian."[6] I wanted to be the kind of Christian woman whose life lived out (to *some* extent, at least!) the divine transformation that was taking place on the inside. I well remember tackling God's high calling on my conduct—more specifically my speech—in these two specific ways.

- *Speak of the Lord.* One day I paused on the patio at my church to chat with a woman I hadn't visited with for a while. In seconds I recognized that this was not the usual exchange of pleasantries that one generally enjoys on Sunday mornings at church. Nor was it a meaningless encounter or the lame sharing of trivia! No, I was in the presence of a woman whose words left me truly energized spiritually and inspired me to want to rush home, curl up with my Bible for the afternoon, and spend time with the Lord.

  Well, as I walked away, I asked the Lord to please help me put my finger on what this woman did or said that had impacted me to the core. As I reviewed our time together and sorted out the particulars, I soon realized that *she spoke of the Lord*. Of course she spoke of other things, too—practical things. After all, it was a conversation! But somehow she blessed God with her every breath. She exalted Him and brought Him to the forefront of our discussion. It was as if *He* was right there with us (as indeed He was and always is)—the center of our talk—at least from her side of our discussion. Yes, she spoke out of a full heart, a heart full of Him!

And so this humbled woman (me—yes, I was convicted) and this excited woman (me again— oh, how I wanted the enthusiasm for God that she had, and oh, how I wanted to have the same effect on others that she had on me, to move them to include the Lord in their every thought) went home, curled up with my Bible, spent time with my Lord...and made a decision. I made a decision *to speak of the Lord*, to begin as many sentences as possible with the words "The Lord..." or "God..." In essence, I was making a decision to put Him first. Oh, He's first in my heart, but I wanted Him to be first in my talk, too!

I'm certainly not there yet, but I daily ask God to help me share His goodness with those I talk to. As the psalmist announced, "I will praise You, O LORD, with my whole heart; I will tell of all Your marvelous works" (Psalm 9:1). And, as he instructs elsewhere, "Let the redeemed of the LORD say so..." (Psalm 107:2). That's what I want for us, that we would speak of the Lord.

- *Speak well of others.* Another decision I've made as a woman who desires to answer God's high calling to godliness and behavior that speaks well of Him (Titus 2:5) is that I will not participate in gossip. Gossip and slander are definitely *not* what you would expect to come out of the mouth of a woman who is busy worshiping God in her heart! And it's *not* what you would expect to come out of the mouth of an "older woman" whose role and assignment from God is to love and help the other women in the church!

We'll cover some of the how-to's of becoming a woman who speaks well of others in our next two chapters as God, through the apostle Paul, issues yet another high calling—the older women are not to be slanderers (Titus 2:3). Until then, there's one thing you can do to speak well of others—*don't gossip!*

To Sum It Up...

Whew! I'm sure neither of us doubts for a second that *godliness* is a h-i-g-h calling! It stretches upward! It soars to the heavens! It speaks of God. And yet we are called to live out this godliness here...now...on this earth...in our home, in our work, and in our church.

I've thought much about our attempts in these first two chapters to wrap our arms around the word *godliness,* a word that at once defies definition. At best, to sum it up, I believe you and I must pray for God's grace to nurture on the *inside* what He calls us to live out on the *outside.* By doing so, we display before everyone a behavior that is becoming of a woman who professes to know God. Now that's godly living!

Looking Upward

As we end (for now) this discussion of godliness and how you and I can set our affections on things above and set godly goals, I want to leave you with these two questions. Look inward, dear one, and then look upward.

Are you one of God's younger women? Do you know a "Mary Jane"? Are you on the lookout, watching those who seem to live their life in the shadow of the Almighty? Take in their behavior. Notice their actions. Pay attention to their conduct. Spend time with them if possible. Learn from these dear saints. And emulate all that you find to be Christlike and Godlike. To be sound in faith and holy in life—this is the kernel of Christianity.[7] May this not only be true of those older, godly women you behold....but of you and me!

Are you one of God's older women? Are you a "Mary Jane" who provides your younger sisters in the church with a model of this high calling to reverent behavior? Do your actions reflect a heart that acknowledges God and His presence in all that you do? It is only as your soul is constantly dwelling on the God you love and serve and on His awesome, holy presence that your behavior will show forth your reverence for Him and evoke the same in others. Your state of worship will cause others to think of God too, and will move them to worship right along with you. In other words, they will not be able to be in *your* presence without thinking about *God*.

How can you possibly have this effect on others? As Clement of the Church at Alexandria, Egypt said in the bygone days of the late second century, "The Christian must live as if all life were a sacred assembly."[8] This is indeed a tall challenge for those of us who love the Lord and live to serve Him in all that we do. And yet God has placed just such a calling upon our lives as His women, and He has placed it first on His essential "to-do" and "to-be" list for us in Titus 2:3-5—we are to be reverent in our behavior.

Essential 2

"the older women [are to] be...not slanderers"
—TITUS 2:3

"As we consider the essentials for godly living that the Bible brings to us as women, we must first of all desire what God in His wisdom and grace calls us to."

"Second, we must beseech God for His able help as we reach and stretch and seek for the reality of these divine elements of our high calling. And godly speech is one of them."

Chapter Three

A Woman's High Calling to Godly Speech

*H*ang on, dear one. We're going for a ride! And what a ride it is! Along the way, we'll recognize another high calling from God on our lives.

In our last two chapters we tasted a little bit of heaven on earth, didn't we? We looked at godliness and godly behavior. We spoke of priestesses, of cathedrals, and of a few of "the holy women" of old (1 Peter 3:5), women such as Anna who approached all of life as an opportunity to worship. We also encountered Elizabeth and Mary, who evidenced with their actions and their words exactly where their hearts were— riveted on God and in God. We might say that we went to the heights of holiness as we entertained God's high calling to worship and to worshipful behavior. We went to heaven, as it were, witnessing and wondering at the godly conduct God calls His women to—His calling to exhibit behavior that is godly, reverent, pious, and sacred, and moves others to think of God too.

But now, prepare yourself, my friend. We're going to descend into hell itself! In this chapter we drop from the heights of heaven and holiness down to the depths of the evils of the devil himself. Instead of moving others to worship, we witness the harm and evil done to others when we gossip about them and slander them. Our next high calling from God is that we *be not slanderers* (Titus 2:3).

God's Calling to Godly Speech

Just to briefly review, our first essential calling from God is to godliness. We, as women of God, are summoned to "be reverent in behavior" (Titus 2:3). We are to conduct ourselves in a manner that reflects God at the center of our lives. Our behavior is to be godly and should testify to our holiness. That means our heart is to be devoted to God, our mind is to be dwelling on Him, and our lips are to speak of Him. Such a preoccupation with the Lord will permeate our behavior, our speech, our manner, and even our appearance and our movements.

And now, Paul, after pointing to the *positive*—to reverent, godly behavior—next approaches a *negative.* He writes to Titus, a pastor on the island of Crete, that the women in the church (and, more specifically, the older women) are not to be slanderers. They are not to be malicious gossips. Perhaps his thinking went like this—"If these women are to be the models and teachers for the younger women, how could they *help* other women if they are *hindering* them by gossiping about them?!"

I'm sure you're getting the picture: the two—godliness and maliciousness—just do not go together! Our God-ordained role of *serving* and the act of *slandering* are extreme opposites.

So, if God doesn't want you and me to gossip or slander or malign others, then we'd better learn exactly what slander is and exactly how to follow His calling to us to "be...not slanderers" (Titus 2:3).

Learning About Gossip

Unlike the words used in the New Testament for reverent behavior (which we discovered are used only once), *slanderer* is used many times. And it has a frightening meaning! The biblical word *slanderer* comes from a Greek word *diabolos* and means malicious gossip, slanderer, or false accuser. It points to bringing charges against another, and usually with hostile intent.

But here's the really ugly side of the word: *diabolos* is used...

- thirty-four (that's 34!) times in the New Testament as a title for Satan—(as the Bible reports in Revelation 12:10, "Satan is the accuser of the brethren")

- one time regarding Judas, Jesus' disciple who betrayed Him—(Jesus called Judas "a devil" in John 6:70)

- one time to describe the behavior of hardened unbelievers in the end times (2 Timothy 3:3)

- two other times, in reference to women, that can be literally translated "she-devil"—(here in Titus 2:3 and again in 1 Timothy 3:11)

Not very good company, is it? I mean, slandering, gossiping women who are called to godliness and to holiness and to godly behavior...lumped in with Satan, Judas, and hardened unbelievers? As James exclaimed elsewhere, "These things ought not to be so" (James 3:10)!

No, they "ought not." And so God in His Word calls you and me away from such evil. In Titus 2:3, as well as in 1 Timothy 3:11, we are called to be "not slanderers"..."not scandalmongers"..."not given to intrigue"..."avoiding scandal." We are to be women who are not "given to slandering," "who will not talk scandal," women "saying no evil of others."[1]

Instead, my sister who aspires to godliness, God calls us to His higher standard. He calls us to grow up in this matter of the mouth, to mature in speech, to strive for *godly* speech. And He declares that those women who are older in age and in their relationship with the Lord (Titus 2:3) and those women who are in some leadership capacity in the local church (1 Timothy 3:11) are to use their tongues for ministering goodness instead of gossiping. As Dr. Gene Getz writes about this distinctive mark of maturity in his book *The Measure of a Woman*, "How we use our tongues serves as a precise measurement of our Christian maturity....How we use our tongues reflects on everything we do and affects everything we do, and every person we come in contact with."[2]

Aspiring to Godly Speech

I hope and pray that you, dear one, are as struck by these awful definitions of slandering as I am. And I trust that you are as moved to follow after God's high calling to godly speech as I am. I know that learning the truth and the facts about gossip has been life-changing for me as I've desired for at least two decades to put away gossip and to grow in this all-important area of godly speech instead. It hasn't been—and still isn't—easy, but I'm committed to God's goal of godly speech and to making the effort day by day. My reasoning (and perhaps Paul's as well) goes something like this as I read Paul's words to those ladies who are to teach and lead and serve the other women in the church:

How could a woman of maturity involve herself in such evil works as slandering and maligning and destroying others? *Answer?* She couldn't. Because godly speech is a mark of her maturity.

How could a woman who is engaged in the work of our loving Lord purposefully harm even one of His dear sheep for whom He died? *Answer?* She couldn't. Because godly speech is a mark of her maturity.

How could a woman of dignity, a "holy" woman, a godly woman, a woman in a constant state of worship, utter a slanderous word against a person created in the image of the God she worships? *Answer?* She couldn't. Because godly speech is a mark of her maturity.

As she is constantly worshiping, she is constantly praying, "Let the words of my mouth...be acceptable in Your sight, O LORD, my strength and my redeemer" (Psalm 19:14). And gossip, as you and I both know, is *not* acceptable in the sight of the Lord. In fact, as we'll soon see, His Word teaches us that He hates it!

Life-Lessons Learned from Others

Sadly, the Bible shows us many women who participated in the demise of others through ungodly, unbridled, and slanderous speech. For instance,

> *Potiphar's wife*—lied to her husband and falsely accused the righteous Joseph. What was the outcome of her malicious, slanderous report? God's servant Joseph spent about three years in prison (Genesis 39).

Jezebel—set into motion the false accusal of the righteous Naboth for the sin of blaspheming God and her husband, the king. The result? Naboth was stoned to death (1 Kings 21).

Martha—too, was guilty of maligning both her sister and her Lord. She accused Mary, saying she "has left me to serve alone." And of Jesus she railed, "Lord, do You not care...?" (Luke 10:41). Each was a defaming comment and attacked the character of another.

Oh, may it never be reported of you and me, women to whom God puts forth His high calling to godly speech, that we harmed another through gossip and slander!

The Facts About Gossip

Before we move on to the *how-to's* of this essential of godly speech in the next chapter, there are a few additional facts we need to know about *un*-godly speech. Take note of this information from the Bible:

The Source of Gossip—As we learned earlier, the devil is the source of slander and malicious gossip. The seriousness of gossip is instantly understood when we (once again!) acknowledge that the word *slanderer* is used in the New Testament as a title for Satan.

The Causes of Gossip—Here are a few of the more obvious causes of gossip.

First is *an evil heart*. Coming from Satan, there's no doubt that gossip is evil. But Jesus also pointed His finger at an evil heart when He explained, "A good man out of the good treasure of his heart brings forth good; and an evil man out of the evil treasure of his heart brings forth evil. For out of the abundance of the heart his mouth speaks" (Luke 6:45).

Second on our list of causes is *hatred*. David complained to God, "They have also surrounded me with words of hatred" (Psalm 109:3).

Third is plain ole *foolishness*. This is one cause that really makes me think twice about gossip! Proverbs, the book of wisdom, states that "whoever spreads slander is a fool" (Proverbs 10:18). I work very hard at "wisdom," at praying for it, at reaching for it, at attaining it, keeping it, using it, and at becoming more of a woman of wisdom. And it's shocking to realize that every time I gossip, I have just declared myself to be a fool!

And fourth is *idleness*. Paul knew this. And he exhorted his protégé Timothy to make sure the women in the church at Ephesus were not idle. He wrote (to Timothy and to us!) to beware lest "they learn to be idle, wandering about from house to house, and not only idle but also gossips and busybodies, saying things which they ought not" (1 Timothy 5:13).

I hope you're beginning to understand—to "see"!—why we as women who possess God's high calling to godly speech can have nothing to do with gossip and slander! Our high calling from God to god-liness and good-liness, to maturity and usefulness, to becoming the lovely, dignified, older, wiser, female saints in the body of Christ, leaves no place for an evil heart, hatred, foolishness, or idleness.

The Public Consequences of Gossip—Plus, there are disastrous consequences when we gossip. Just look at what God says happens to relationships among His people and in His church when someone chooses to gossip!

- Gossip separates friends. *Everyone* has tasted the pain of a friendship that's soured because of gossip! And some awful-but-true truths about this fact come to us from (again!) the wisdom book of Proverbs. "A whisperer separates the best of friends" (Proverbs 16:28), and "he [or she] who repeats a matter separates the best of friends" (Proverbs 17:9).

- Gossip causes strife. Proverbs explains in riddle-like fashion that "where there is no wood, the fire goes out; and where there is no talebearer, *strife* ceases" (Proverbs 26:20, emphasis added). Here God paints for us a word picture of logs and a fire, one fueling the other. And, just as fuel feeds a fire, so gossip feeds trouble and creates a "fire" of strife.

- Gossip causes discord in the body of Christ. Proverbs also points out the distressing reality that gossip—"a lying tongue" and "a false witness who speaks lies"—sows discord and creates divisions "among brethren" (Proverbs 6:17,19). (And, by the way, this proverb also reports that these things are considered by God to be "an abomination to Him"—verse 16!)

- Gossip is the same as murder. The end result of gossip's evil is murder. The Old Testament king David acknowledged, "For I hear the slander of many;…While they take counsel together against me, they scheme to take away my life" (Psalm 31:13). Wouldn't you agree, after what we've just seen from the Bible, that gossip kills? It kills friendships, ministries, people, leaders, marriages, reputations, and even churches.

And the conclusion? Never, never, *never*, should one of God's beautiful and reverent and godly women be a part of separating friends, causing strife and division in the church, nor be a partner in murder!

The Personal Consequences of Gossip—But there's still another adverse consequence to gossip, and that is what it does to the gossiper! Yes, others are hurt. But you and I are hurt too when we slander others. How?

- Gossip jeopardizes our ministry. Our position and opportunities as ministers among women diminish when we injure the very ones we are to instruct. We are called by God to be helpers of women, teachers of women, encouragers of women (Titus 2:3-5). That ministry ceases when the words out of our own mouths wound others and disqualify us from ministering to others.

- Gossip harms us. When you and I gossip, my friend, we incur a huge loss. What kind of loss? We suffer the loss of character, the loss of respect, the loss of high regard, and the loss of dignity, not to mention the loss of spiritual growth and usefulness. As an old proverb says, "Let not your tongue cut your throat!" A modern translation of these words might be, "People who have sharp tongues often end up cutting their own throats."

- Gossip can never be taken back. There's not a person alive who hasn't felt the fatal effects of gossip! And no matter how much you apologize or try to make it right with someone you've discredited, the harm and hurt still remain—you have smeared and stained the reputation of another. It's a true saying that "a wound from the tongue is worse than a wound from the sword." That's the message of Proverbs 12:18—"There is one who speaks like the piercings of a sword, but the tongue of the wise promotes health." Are your words about others healing...or harmful?

Hopefully our look at these atrocious consequences—both public and personal—has shown both of us vividly (once again!) the satanic source and the evil of gossip! I know it's been a sobering reminder for me.

Looking Upward

Well, this has turned into quite a lesson, hasn't it? I know I've tried to share with women through my books[3] about my own struggles in this area of gossip and ungodly speech. Indeed, the nurturing of godly speech and the elimination of ungodly speech has become a lifetime goal for me! And I want you to make this essential of *godly speech* a lifetime goal for you, too.

As we consider the essentials for godly living that the Bible teaches us as women, I want both of us to, first of all, desire what God in His wisdom and grace calls us to. And then I want us to beseech God for His able help as we reach and stretch and seek for the reality of these elements of our high calling. And godly speech is one of these elements.

As we look upward to this particular high calling to godly speech, we can't help but be struck by the perfect compassion and care of Jesus for others. Oh, to be like Jesus, who

Himself was pure and holy love! And oh, to be like Jesus, whose lips spoke no sin (1 Peter 2:22)! Yes, He confronted sin. And, yes, He called men and women to a better life, to better behavior. But He helped. He touched. He healed. He bettered the lives of others.

This, dear one, is our high calling—*not* to do the dastardly work of the devil, *not* to be a "she-devil" as it were—but to be like Jesus. We are called by God in His Word to minister and to serve and to assist and to help and to better the lives of others. And certainly, no life has ever been bettered by gossip and slander! So let's do something else God calls us to do—let's lay aside all malice and all evil speaking (1 Peter 2:1) and instead love one another (John 13:34).

Essential
2

"the older women [are to] be...not slanderers"
—TITUS 2:3

"She opens her mouth with wisdom,
And on her tongue is the law of kindness."
—PROVERBS 31:26

"If we love—love the Lord, love His Word, love
His people, love one another, and love His
women—then we don't and won't gossip.
God calls us as His women to 'be...not
slanderers' (Titus 2:3), but to love instead.
Won't you look upward, upward to Him, for His
help, as you follow after this high-but-practical,
everyday calling from Him to godly speech?"

Chapter Four

Godly Speech—An Essential for Godly Living

I am so blessed to have several women in my life and in my church who model for me and others God's high calling not only to godly behavior, but also to godly speech. So, before we head into the nuts and bolts of pursuing and practicing God's goal of godly speech, I want to take a few minutes to describe these ladies to you so that we can both benefit from their modeling.

Meet Some of My Sisters

My thoughts go first to Loretta, a long-time "older woman" friend and influence in my life. I can see her right now in my mind's eye, standing in the aisle at church, or near the coffee table at Bible study, or in the foyer of our church, standing there in all her purity and guilelessness. (No, she doesn't have a halo, but a glow is there nevertheless, a mark of the Lord at work in her life.) She literally radiates love—love from her eyes, love from her manner, love from her touch, love from the shelter of her arms as they embrace me in a genuine hug, love from her words as they caress me and do their work of building me up and binding up any wounds, and love from her heart as she expresses her concern for me.

And then there's Mary. The word "ditto" comes to mind! Just last week after I taught at our women's Bible study, I looked up and there she was, purposefully coming across the room. Even her eyes reached out to me, eyes filled with sparkling love, even filled with a few tears due to her loving concern and sincere desire to help in any way. And, of course, her arms were reaching out too with a hug and a pat. And out of her mouth? What would you expect from a "godly" woman? Sure enough, she spoke the words we all need most—words of encouragement, words of praise, personal words about something she'd noticed or seen in me. This particular week, she grabbed me with both hands and looked me straight in the eyes, smiled, and stated, "You just get better and better." I tell you, her love and strength in the Lord was transferred directly from Him...through her...right into me! And, oh, did I ever need it! And there it was—from the Source (God)...to the giver (Mary)...to the recipient (me).

And then there's Nina. Nina doesn't say much. But she'll always inquire, "How are you? How's Jim? How are Katherine and Courtney [our daughters]? How are your little grandbabies?" Nina always assures me that she is praying for me. And then, almost weekly or at least monthly, a treasured note of love and encouragement and affirmation arrives in the mail, along with assurances of faithful prayer and several scriptures acknowledging the certainty of God's steadfast love and faithfulness.

And then there's Emarie, the encourager. If I said, "Ditto again," would you be getting the picture, dear reader? These precious older saints are examples to me and to countless others. Their hearts are always welcoming. Their arms are always open. Their love is always overflowing. Their ears are ever ready to listen. And their lips are there to be used to not only affirm, but to give wise counsel and encouragement in the Lord. They truly open their lips with wisdom and on their tongues is the law of kindness (Proverbs 31:26)! In the presence of these ladies, only good occurs. One is safe, for one has found a lover and a helper in them.

How I thank God that the hearts and hands and lips of such women are dedicated to helping and encouraging their fellow sisters in the faith, instead of judging them and slandering them. Rather than being petty, censorious, and bitter, these mature-in-the-Lord saints truly use their voices for far better things!

Well, now that I've shared the goal and the beauty that *these* women exhibit through their much-needed ministries and that God also calls you and me to (Titus 2:3-5), let's eagerly turn to the issue of *our* behavior!

A Moment of Review

And just to catch ourselves up, please remember that in the previous chapter we looked at the harm that gossip and slander inflict on the one gossiped about. We also noted the harm that these two evils do to the one who's gossiping.

Well, you and I both know that a third party is also affected, and that is the one who *hears* the gossip. That person, too, pays a high price, because once information is spoken about someone else, the one who hears that information must then do something with it. She must try to forget it, try to disregard it, try to bury it from her own mind and memory...and try not to pass it on! In addition, she must try not to believe it, try not to let it sway her opinion of that person, along with trying not to let it sway her opinion of the person from whom she heard it!

On and on surge the ripples of repercussion that begin when someone gossips. Indeed, they are virtually never ending. And we both know that a word of gossip can never be retracted. And the damage a word of gossip can do is inestimable!

When my husband Jim teaches on the topic of slander, he always shares this favorite story that depicts its far-reaching effects.

> Two friends were inseparable. One day one of them heard a story about his friend, believed it without making enquiries as to its truth, and passed it on. As it went, it grew. His friend heard of it, and their friendship was broken. The man thus maligned was taken seriously ill and lay on his deathbed. His friend who had spread the slander heard of his illness and came to see him, confess his wrong, and ask his forgiveness, which was readily given by the dying man.
>
> "Now," said the dying man, "I want you to do something for me. Take my feather pillow and scatter the feathers in the garden." Though he thought it a strange request, the visitor carried it out and returned to his friend's bedside. "Now," said the dying man, "go and gather the feathers up again."
>
> "That is impossible," said the other.
>
> "Just so," said the wronged man. "I frankly and willingly forgive you for scattering those stories about me, but even my forgiveness cannot revoke the evil that has been done. Slanderous stories scattered abroad cannot be recalled."[1]

Moving Forward

As I promised, this chapter will be the practical part of our study of God's essential of godly speech. So let's begin with a positive goal: I want you to make godly speech a lifetime goal. I know that it's certainly one of mine. Proverbs 31:26 just happens to be one of my passionate goals for life. Here God, through the gracious and lovely Proverbs 31 woman, teaches us two guidelines for our speech:

> She opens her mouth with *wisdom*, and
> on her tongue is the law of *kindness*.

So I want to ask you to make both *wisdom* and *kindness* lifelong studies and goals. You may even want to write out such a goal. Compose a heartfelt commitment to the Lord. Dedicate yourself to such a worthy goal. Pray daily to be on guard. And look to God for His grace to make the choices that prove your desire to pursue God's high calling of godly speech.

I once read this interesting parallel.

> When a young doctor graduates and before he begins to practice medicine, he takes the Hippocratic oath, and part of that oath is a pledge never to repeat anything that he has heard in the house of a patient, or anything that he has heard about a patient, even if he has heard it on the street.[2]

Don't you wish that we as women in the church were required by God to take such an oath? I even wish we could sign something, a pledge, a covenant of some sort (such as John Wesley's covenant at the end of this chapter). That might make us think more seriously about our slanderous words. Christ did not say, "Go ye, therefore, into all the world and preach the *gossip*." No, He said instead that we are to go into all the world and preach the *gospel*, the Good News of Jesus Christ, the truth of His love that led Him to die for us (Matthew 28:19-20).

When Paul wrote to Titus that the older women in the church were not to be gossips (Titus 2:3), women in the work of the Lord were expected to be engaged in acts of love. Only a woman could properly perform certain acts of kindness (then and now) for another woman—instructing the female converts, assisting them in baptism, in childbirth, in counseling, etc. And while working among these younger Christians, these ministering women could easily hear and then repeat gossip, causing damage to the very person they were to help.

Again, as I've said before (and plead with you now), women who are supposed to be performing loving and helping ministries in the church must not gossip! The two are opposites. How can we be loving and murdering at the same time? It would be as pathetic as a surgeon who, after painstakingly spending ten hours in surgery, deliberately prescribes medication that poisons and sooner or later causes the death of his patient!

No, the woman who is meant to minister to her sisters-in-Christ must not allow herself to be either a receptacle or a vehicle of gossip and scandal.

Are you wondering *how?* Good! Let's go on!

Making Progress

Don't you agree, in light of what we're learning, that it's "essential" that we work at making progress in obeying Paul's command that we be not slanderers? Whenever I teach on this subject of godly speech, I'm usually asked questions like the following. I'll share the questions...and a list of my own personal "how-to's" regarding the issue of gossip.

Question #1—"How can I avoid gossiping?"

- Think godly thoughts about others. Philippians 4:8 gives us God's standard for godly *thinking*: whatever things are true...noble...just...pure... lovely...of good report, if there is any virtue and if there is anything praiseworthy—meditate on these things.

- If any of your thoughts about others don't measure up to these biblical guidelines, they must be confessed and dealt with as sin. And the sooner, the better!

- Agree with your closest friends not to gossip. Share with them your desire to grow in this area. Tell them about your new goals and the parameters you've set. Also ask them to let you know when you've slipped.

- Avoid (or at least be armed and on your toes!) those settings that tend to lend themselves to gossip (luncheons, parties, showers, and even meetings). I like, instead, to be with groups of women in a Bible study or in a discipleship setting, where the aim is spiritual growth and exposure to God's Word and God's truths.

- Avoid women who engage in gossip. You'll find that, unfortunately, there are certain women who regularly gossip and are even somewhat skillful at drawing others—including *you*—into it.

- Never name names. I'll say more about this in a minute when I repeat it, but it's a good guideline.

- Say nothing. And that means *say nothing!* If your mouth is closed, it's hard to gossip!

Question #2—"How can I work at eliminating gossip from my life?"

I think these four *T*'s will help. I know I try to live by them.

T ime—Idle time can create many an opportunity to gossip! So have a schedule that is tight (even to the minute!) and keeps you running (even breathlessly!). Then you won't have *time* to talk or to gossip or to listen to gossip (see 1 Timothy 5:13)!

T elephone—Let your telephone answering machine handle your calls. Then, like an efficient executive, return your calls at 11:30 A.M. and again at 4:30 P.M. (I find that most women are gearing up for lunch or dinner at these times, and often can't even remember why they called in the first place!) Handling your telephone calls in this way tends to put you in the driver's seat of both timing and topic of conversation. Of course there are those dear souls who need your comfort, your word in season (Isaiah 50:4), your sunshine call. Give *them* all the time they need. But beware of aimlessly chattering away on the phone! When you talk on the phone, preface your calls with something like, "I just have a minute. How can I help you?"

And don't initiate too many phone calls. See if there's any other way to communicate and accomplish your goals. That's one reason I love e-mail. Cell phones, too, are great for making quick calls. The reception is never very good, so you tend to get quickly to the point and get your business done! Over...and out!

I also keep a liberal supply of postcards a nd notecards for little words of encouragement or communications that I wish to send, or for small matters of business. You can also ask someone else to call your committee or group with reminders.

*T*alk—When you do talk, don't talk too long. Do you have one of those little three-minute hourglass-shaped egg timers? You know, the kind with the sand in it, that you turn upside-down to time exactly three minutes? If not, get one at your local kitchen store. And while you're at it, get one to go beside each telephone in your house! And just in case you can't find one, you can simply be faithful to use your kitchen timer. I especially love my husband's phone—it tells you the length of each and every call...*while* you are talking. It just keeps right on counting until you hang up! Now, there's a visual aid worth its price! Whatever method(s) you use, the point is clear—less is best. As the proverb teaches us, "In the multitude of words sin is not lacking, but he who restrains his lips is wise" (Proverbs 10:19).

*T*arry—You don't have to quickly answer every question you're asked. And you don't have to answer them on the spot. You can always ask for time to think and pray about things *before* (and *if!*) you answer. A hasty answer is usually a foolish answer (Proverbs 29:20)!

Question #3—"How can I make permanent changes in the way that I talk?"

It sure helps me to remember these basic truths and tactics!

1. Remember the source of slander—the devil.

2. Realize the causes—hatred, jealousy, envy, an evil eye and heart.

3. Choose your company carefully—Isolate yourself, if you must, until *you* get it right. Then step out again.

4. Choose your activities carefully—Be busy...too busy...to talk on the phone, to go to lunch, to sit for hours in the dorm, to "hang out" with the girls. Take a class instead, run your errands, read a book, or even write a book!!!!

5. Never mention names—Why? Because anytime you tell a story about someone and give their name, you put yourself in a position for someone else to say, "I heard Elizabeth talking about so-and-so the other day." Or, "Elizabeth said this about so-and-so...." and then off they go on their own interpretation or rendition or slanted report of what you said. Even your good words can be distorted by another.

6. Praise only—Be known as a woman who is a friend of women, who finds the good in others, who loves her sisters-in-Christ (or her sisters-in-flesh, or her mother or her mother-in-law).

7. Pray—for yourself in this area. Also pray for those who harm you. This way you are telling the right Person—God—about your woes. *His* job is to vindicate the righteous and to avenge those who wrong them (Romans 12:19). *Your* job is to pray and to forgive. I just read this morning these instructive words from writer/teacher *par*

excellence, Chuck Swindoll: "Trust me on this one...you'll never regret forgiving someone who doesn't deserve it!"[3] Plus, praying for our enemies is one way to love them (Luke 6:27-28).

8. Deal with gossip as sin—Acknowledge that you have a problem, confess it as sin, and tell God all about it (1 John 1:8-9).

Question #4— "What should I do when others gossip?"

1. Leave the scene—Joseph in the Old Testament shows us vividly how to flee from sin (Genesis 39:12)! So flee! Leave the room! Get out! ASAP! Excuse yourself. Go get a breath of fresh air. Make a phone call. "Powder your nose." Just get out—even if it's for a minute. And while you're out of earshot, shoot up a prayer to God. Ask Him for His wisdom about the best way to handle the situation. Then, perhaps as the figure of the three little monkeys that resided on my grand-mother's mantle demonstrates, you will "Hear no evil, see no evil, speak no evil."

2. Declare your discomfort—Speak up. Say some-thing like, "I'm sorry, maybe it's me, but I'm not comfortable with this conversation. Could we please change the subject (or move on with our lesson)?"

3. Guard your facial expressions—Unfortunately, we can "gossip" or plant seeds of doubt or smear someone's reputation without a word. How? By the use of our face and eyes. Who hasn't won-dered when someone rolled their eyes, or shook their head, or raised their eyebrows in a knowing manner, or grimaced at the mention of another's

name? Be sure you don't communicate negatively about people in these telltale ways.

4. Be ready with a positive phrase or two—I like to take the person's side and come to the aid of the one being maligned. For instance, I'll say, "Oh, no! Bless her heart!" "Oh, we must pray for her!" "Oh, she must be suffering!" "Oh, that just *couldn't* be true! She's too kind to do something like that."

    Another kind of phrase comes out when I hear words like, "Don't tell anyone, but..." At that point, I raise both hands and interrupt with, "Well, don't tell me!"

5. And again, say nothing. Enough said!

Looking Upward

If you don't mind, I'd like to use this section of our chapter to add two more "how-to's" to help us keep from gossiping. It certainly fits under the heading of *Looking Upward!*

*   Use your tongue to glorify God—After all, the tongue was created to glorify the Lord. To gossip and slander is to pervert its use for that which is ungodly.

*   Nurture a heart of love—As I just read over the descriptions of my precious older women again, I was struck by the number of times I used the word *love*. Perhaps that's the secret, dear one. If we *love*—love the Lord, love His Word, love His people, love one another, and love His women— then we don't and won't gossip. God calls us as

His women to "be...not slanderers" (Titus 2:3), but to love instead. Won't you look upward, upward to Him, for His help, as you follow after this high-but-practical, everyday calling from Him?

Did you know that backbiting and talebearing were considered to be cardinal sins by the early Methodists? John Wesley handwrote these "Six Points of Methodism," which was then signed as a covenant by the fathers of Methodism:

1. That we will not listen to or inquire after any ill concerning each other.

2. That if we hear any ill concerning each other we will not be in a hurry to believe it.

3. That as soon as possible we will communicate what we hear, by speaking to or writing to the person concerned.

4. That until we have done this we will not write or speak a syllable of it to any other person whatsoever.

5. That neither will we mention it, after we have done this, to any other person whatsoever.

6. That we will make no exceptions to these rules, unless we think ourselves absolutely obliged in conscience to do so.[4]

"Can you guess who I am?" was the query at the head of a magazine article. Then followed the description that provided the clue and answer:

"I have no respect for justice and no mercy for defenseless humanity. I ruin without killing. I tear down homes. I break hearts and wreck lives. You will find me in the pews of the pious as well as in the haunts of the unholy. I gather strength with age. I have made my way where greed, distrust, and dishonor are unknown; yet my victims are as numerous as the sands of the sea, and often as innocent. *My name is Gossip*."[5]

Essential

*"the older women [are to] be...not given
to much wine"*
—TITUS 2:3

*"It has been well said that the future is with the
disciplined, and that quality has been placed
first...for without it the other gifts, however great,
will never realize their maximum potential.
Only the disciplined person will rise to
his highest powers."*
—J. OSWALD SANDERS

*"Personal discipline is a most powerful
character quality and one worthy of dedicating
your life to nurturing."*

Chapter Five

A Woman's High Calling to Personal Discipline

When I think of personal discipline, I can't help but think of one particular afternoon this past Christmas season. I had been on a shopping outing to gather up the appropriate gifts for my husband Jim and for our two daughters, two sons-in-law, and two new infant grandbabies. As I headed up the major boulevard that leads to our home, the car radio was tuned to one of our Los Angeles 24-hour news stations. The news story for the hour just happened to be about *who* spends the money in most U.S. families.

Do you know *who* that person is? Well, my friend, it's *you* and *me! Women* are the major spenders in America.

The report went on to give statistics about the percentage of household income we women spend, the amounts (in the billions of dollars!) we charge on credit cards, and our purchasing habits on (and including our addictions to) home shopping networks. To our shame, the sordid and revealing facts and figures went on and on. Finally, the news story ended with predictions of how much money and how many purchases female consumers were anticipated to make on the Internet during the upcoming Christmas season.

It was *not* a very flattering profile! (And you can be sure that I felt a tinge of conviction as I had just been out and done exactly what the news story was reporting on!)

That incident did help me focus anew on the need for yet another essential for godly living for you and me as God's women—His high calling to personal discipline. I know this particular calling has been a challenge to me for almost three decades. But I can also say that, as I continue to heed God's calling to self-control and temperance and discipline in every area of my life, remarkable changes have occurred in my habits, accompanied by tremendous growth and maturity.

Personal discipline, dear one, is a most powerful character quality and one worthy of dedicating your life to nurturing. J. Oswald Sanders wrote about the significance of discipline and the required need to continually develop it in his classic book *Spiritual Leadership*.

It has been well said that the future is with the disciplined, and that quality has been placed first...for without it the other gifts, however great, will never realize their maximum potential. Only the disciplined person will rise to his highest powers. He is able to lead because he has conquered himself.[1]

Considering God's Calling to Personal Discipline

Exactly what is this high calling to personal discipline? We know that it is yet another essential for godly living. We also know that God places it third on His list of qualities for the older women in the church: "the older women likewise, that they be reverent in behavior, not slanderers, *not given to much wine...*" (Titus 2:3, emphasis added).

As we seek to understand discipline as an essential for godly living, I would like to treat it from two sides—the negative and the positive—and from two passages of scripture that speak to us as women. I want to draw the negative side of our definition for personal discipline—what we are *not* to do—from our passage here in Titus 2:3. And I want to draw the positive side of our definition for personal discipline— what we *are to do* and *to be* instead—from Paul's exhortation for women in the church as stated in 1 Timothy 3:11.

First the *negative*. As I quoted above, the Bible states that the older women are *not* to be "given to much wine" (Titus 2:3). Another version translates Titus 2:3 as *not* "enslaved to much wine" (NASB). Yet another warns that the women should "beware of becoming slaves to drink."[2] As Dr. Charles Ryrie observes, "Apparently some of the older women were given to gossiping and drinking."[3] And here in Titus 2:3, Paul has just landed with both feet on both vices. He wants these two behaviors—gossiping and drinking—eliminated from the lives of the Lord's ladies.

Next the *positive*. Instead of being enslaved to wine (Titus 2:3), God wants His women to "be...temperate" (1 Timothy 3:11), to be free from addiction. Other translations of 1 Timothy 3:11 call us to be *sober, to be controlling [our]selves*, and *to be women of self-control*.[4] As one scholar explains, to be sober means "literally being sober...primarily in a physical sense, as opposed to excess in drink, but passing into the general sense of self-control and equanimity."[5]

So then, to summarize, on the negative side you and I are *not to be* enslaved to wine (or anything else), and on the positive side we *are to be* sober-minded women of self-control instead.

Considering the Problem

Are you wondering why sobriety and the use of wine was such a concern in the church? The answer lies in the pagan religions that existed during the days of Paul and Titus that were centered on drunken worship. The people communed with their false gods while drunk with wine, a fact my husband Jim and I witnessed firsthand when we visited the ruins in modern-day Lebanon of a huge temple designed for just such worship.

The dilapidated structure of the temple of Baalbek overlooks vast grain fields and flourishing vineyards. It was a pretty site for a building, but what went on inside that ancient edifice was *not* pretty! This temple was devoted to the worship of Dionysus, whose domain was "the liquid fire in the grape." As worshipers, both male and female drank freely of the potent, abundant wine from the grain fields and vineyards, their worship turning into "dancing madness" and "orgies."[6]

This, dear reader, is the backdrop against which Paul lays down his instruction that the women in the church were not to be "given to" or users of much wine. Clearly the primary meaning of his admonishment is that no Christian woman is to be enslaved to wine, that no woman in the church is to be brought under bondage to wine or to become the servant of wine. That's what it says and that's what it means.

Paul, along with the other apostles, strongly believed that Christianity *must* and *could* deliver all believers from bondage to wine.[7] And he also believed that women in their old age *must* and *should* be examples to their younger sisters in sobriety.

Considering the Meaning

But personal discipline and temperance is more than a call to abstain from alcoholic excess. *Much* more! God's women are to maintain self-control and mastery in *every* area of their life. We are to be calm, dispassionate, grave, and sober. We are to live in a manner that is characterized by moderation and restraint *in all things* and *in all areas* of life. We are to be free from excesses in and addiction to *anything*. It's essential for godly living!

Temperate means free from addiction, and looking at its uses in the New Testament will definitely help us to understand this high calling from God upon our lives. So here's a quick run-through.

Who is to possess personal discipline and temperance? The Bible says...

> Pastors, elders, and the overseers of the church are to be temperate (1 Timothy 3:2).

> Women married to these men and/or women assisting in the church are also to be temperate (1 Timothy 3:11).

> The "older" men in the church are to be temperate (Titus 2:2).

What are the biblical admonitions and applications of temperance and discipline?

> We are not to sleep, but are to *watch* and be *sober-minded* (1 Thessalonians 5:6,8). Here Paul tells believers to remain balanced and alert instead of becoming distracted with the world as they wait for the coming of the Lord.

> We are also to *watch* in all things, to be *sober* in all matters (2 Timothy 4:5). Paul charged his young protégé Timothy to be diligent in preaching the gospel even when men refused to

listen and were drawn to the sensationalism and sentimentalities of false teachers and myths. Timothy was to remain calm, steady, and sane, to be *sober*, to *watch* in all things, and to teach sound doctrine.[8]

We are to gird up the loins of our *mind* and be *sober* (1 Peter 1:13). Here Peter admonishes the believers to be sober-minded—to gird up and tie up their thoughts—and to live according to their priorities as Christians. Instead of being distracted and intoxicated by the allurements of the world, they were to be diligently focused on the tasks at hand.

We are to realize that the end is at hand and, therefore, we are to be *sober-minded* and *watching* in prayer (1 Peter 4:7). Rather than sitting and waiting for the end times, we are called to be in a watchful pursuit of holiness.

We are also to be *sober* because of our adversary the devil (1 Peter 5:8). The sober-minded Christian is to be serious and to have a clear understanding of the tactics of the devil—he is like a lion who is ready to pounce on naive, unsuspecting victims.

I hope you noticed the two repeated concepts—watching and sober-mindedness. Yes, we have the joy of the Lord. We Christians, of all people, should be joyous. But we, of all people, should know the dangers of the world and of Satan. Therefore, we are to seek to live a balanced, disciplined life—one of sobriety and vigilance...and one of basking in the joy of the Lord.

What does temperance and self-control mean?

As I considered the ramifications of the scriptures above and what they are teaching us about temperance and the importance of personal discipline and self-control, I also went to my English dictionary for a little help. Putting all things, all meanings, and all definitions together, here's a composite of what temperance and self-control means...

> not addicted to alcoholic beverages (or anything else),
> controlled in our actions and words,
> mild and calm in our emotions,
> lacking in extremes and extravagance, and
> serious in our behavior.

Other descriptions fill out the beautiful meaning of temperance and sober-mindedness. Explanations clearly indicating mental and emotional balance—such as serious and solemn, quiet, not exaggerated, and behavior characterized by reason, sanity, and self-control—help us to grasp the breadth and depth of this wonderful (and much-needed!) quality.

Looking into the Mirror

In our next chapter we'll get into some practicalities and how-to's for making this godly essential of temperance, moderation, and personal discipline a viable quality in our life. However, as we're beginning to get a handle on what this calling from God entails, I think it's time for us to take a look into the mirror and make sure that we are, by God's grace, *doers* of His Word, and not *hearers* only (James 1:22-25).

So, for now, dear one, think about your self-indulgent tendencies for a moment or two. Ask God to help you as we pause to evaluate our behavior and speech patterns and emotions. Honestly consider these questions:

Regarding your use of food and drink or your passions (spending, accumulating possessions, reading matter, television viewing), are there any areas that are excessive or out of control?

Regarding your speech patterns, do you deliberately place restraint upon yourself and your desire to express yourself? Are you pegged as one of the talkative ones, seldom giving others a chance to speak? Or, do you tend to blow up, rant and rave, vent, and emote? Do you lean toward lashing out and screaming at your husband, your children, your siblings, and so on?

Regarding your emotions, is there an excess of heat and fervor and irrationality? Or would you and others characterize you as cool, calm, and collected?

In general, would you describe yourself as excited, agitated, and bothered...or reasonable, rational, and level-headed?

How About an Exercise?

Whenever I teach on these ten essentials that make up God's high calling to His women, I have my students capsulize the meaning of each quality in their own words. Here are just a few of their gleanings and definitions and sayings characterizing temperance and moderation.

A woman who is in control of self, not controlled by self.

A woman who lives a steady lifestyle of self-restraint.

A woman characterized by her ability to keep her appetites, actions, and passions moderate in amount and intensity.

A woman who displays mental and emotional balance.

"*Control* in all things, and control in *all things.*"

"To be calm is a balm."

Why don't you do your own exercise? Consider again the definitions we've looked at for *temperance.* Then see what you can come up with as your own saying or definition. Believe me, it will help you to more earnestly and diligently pursue God's high calling if you understand it for yourself!

Considering Two Questions

Now let's ask...and hopefully answer...two questions about personal discipline for ourselves.

Question #1—Why is this quality an essential for us?

As we've already learned, Paul is referring to ministry in this passage of the Bible, Titus 2:3-5. He has in mind the ministry the older women in the church are to carry on with the younger women. The same is true for you and me—we can greatly minister to those younger than ourselves *if* we are temperate and disciplined and restrained. As women with even-keeled temperaments and self-control, we provide an excellent model to our children and to our younger sisters in the faith.

Plus, such a moderate temper should make us more approachable. Imagine the comfort and confidence another woman would have in approaching us, sensing that there will be no outbursts, no heated arguments, no raised voices, no condemning attitude. (And, because we've grown in the previous quality, there would also be no gossiping about their problem to others!) You see, in order for ministry to occur, others must be able to share their problems with us.

Also, as women possessing the sweet spirit of moderation, we would be able to give fair and sound advice...and to give it calmly! One picture of this quality is that of a courtroom judge (and I'm *not* referring to those seen on TV!). What does such a judge do? He or she sits—"as sober as a judge"—and listens to all of the facts and then calmly and quietly and authoritatively hands down the decision. Without emotion, without partiality, and without a condemning spirit, the judge dispassionately decides what's best. That, dear one, is the way a tempered, disciplined woman ministers to others. Others can always expect the right counsel from us— and without fireworks.

Question #2—Why should we desire to answer this high calling from God?

Imagine the difference such sobriety and discretion and control will make, first of all, in our personal lives! For instance,

- Imagine...being more like Jesus. You and I will be more godly, more like Jesus, and more like the model Paul is writing about in Titus 2 and that God intends for us to be.

- Imagine...enjoying a lifestyle without excesses— in food, in drink, or in any other indulgences! Imagine the trouble we'll bypass as we get our tongue and speech under control! And imagine the financial security we'll gain when we stop spending the money that so many of our passions and habits and indulgences cost!

- Imagine...having a more peaceful lifestyle. I don't know one woman who isn't constantly having to deal with stress and stressful situations. Whether it's busyness or just dealing with daily demands of life, we each must learn to live a godly lifestyle *in* the midst of the whirlwind of life. Oh, to be able to walk through each and every day...and each and every trial that each and every day hurls at us...with balance, with calmness, with a sober mind, and with a frazzle-free head and heart!

- Imagine...impacting the lives of others through greater ministry. And that ministry is extended first and foremost to our own family (Titus 2:4-5). What a blessing we are as wives and mothers and home managers when we're self-controlled! You and I can truly provide a haven of rest for our family when we provide an atmosphere (and provide a wife and a mom!) that contains no screaming. No fits. No anger. No lashing out. No blow-ups. No stomping, slamming, or emoting. How blessed are those who have for a wife or a mother a woman who is serious about answering God's high calling to be steady, calm, rational, and reasonable. Who is cool, calm, and collected. Who has herself under control—even when everything else is falling apart! Who deals with life without agitation or strain, calmly moving into action, solving problems, and doing what is right. And the same goes for your friends, your schoolmates, and your work companions! Your personal discipline and temperance blesses them beyond measure.

- Another "just imagine" just hit me—imagine... being the daughter who grows up in a home and under the shadow and tutelage of a mother who is gentle, steady, quiet, fair, and self-controlled! What a far-reaching, generation-spanning influence such a mother would have!

• Imagine...impacting the women in your church as you model such personal discipline! And believe me, as such a woman, you will never lack for a ministry in the church. You will teach many merely by your example as you walk among the women in your congregation.

Looking Upward

Throughout this chapter we've been describing a woman who seeks to live her life in a dispassionate, disciplined way. Who abstains and refrains. Who is composed and sober-minded and clear-thinking.

But now I'm asking you to do just the opposite—I'm urging you to stir up your passion for godliness and fire up your desire to be all that God calls you to be in this area of personal discipline. I'm asking you to passionately yearn for a *dis*passionate, disciplined life. I'm asking you to passionately long to fulfill God's will for your life in this area of self-control and sober-mindedness. I'm asking you to let loose and dream of blessing those around you at home, at church, and in your community with a countenance and a spirit that remains quiet, no matter what.

I realize that in our present day and age, personal discipline is not exactly a goal many strive for! Perhaps it sounds strict and restrained. Maybe you think it will limit your lifestyle (or at least cramp your style!). But, my dear friend, this is what *God* desires of you and for you. This is what *He* wills for your life. This is the maturity *He* has in mind for you and me as His women. Now, won't you please pray for this passion—a passion for a *dis*passionate, disciplined spirit?

Essential 3

"the older women [are to] be...not given
to much wine"
—TITUS 2:3

"Personal discipline can be as simple as the
two-letter word NO! Christ didn't say, 'Indulge
yourself.' Instead He said, 'Deny yourself'
(Matthew 16:24). So, just say NO!"

"As you discipline your practical life through
planning, your home will turn into more of a
'Home, Sweet Home'! And your life will turn
into more of a 'Life, Sweet Life'! All because of a
measure of personal discipline, sober-
mindedness, moderation, and self-control."

*C*hapter Six

Personal Discipline—An Essential for Godly Living

*W*ell, my friend, it's one thing to pray about, read about, talk about, and think about (even dream about!) personal discipline and the various meanings this habit encompasses—meanings such as moderation, temperance, and sober-mindedness. But as women who desire to heed God's high calling, we've got to take our understanding to another level—a higher level—and look to the Lord for His help in making personal discipline a goal to live by. We must firmly fix this habit into our lives, incorporate it into our behavior, and become known as women who possess personal discipline. In short, we must live by it!

So, for our purposes in this chapter that deals with the practicalities and the how-to's of developing the godly habit of personal discipline in every area of life, I want us to pay heartfelt attention to three areas of life.

Your Physical Life

In God's instructions to us in Titus 2:3, there's no doubt that He is speaking directly to the issue of drinking and intoxication, apparently a serious area of addiction and excess in the churches on Crete. As one reference source notes, this is a "precise reference to drunkenness...[however] it can broaden out to include other forms of self-control."[1]

As we consider our physical life, I want us to encompass all addictions in our discussion of growing in temperance and discipline and self-control. So, exactly what would some areas of excess be? Of course, as Paul points out, alcohol certainly qualifies! I also added several other excesses and addictions for us—food, drugs, spending, possessions, hobbies, sleep, television viewing, and caffeine. (Ouch! *That's* getting a little too close to home for a coffee hound like me!)

We could definitely list many other indulgences, but I want us to focus less on the individual addictions and more on specific ways to gain victory over physical addictions and excesses in general. I want us to work on a *lifestyle* of personal discipline. I'm still growing in this area myself, but here are a few practices that work for me.

1. *Think of models*—I'm not talking about skinny fashion models. I'm not even talking about women who work out at a gym. No, I'm just asking you to think about women you know and admire for their physical discipline, those who exhibit control and mastery over physical passions and cravings.

    For instance, when I think of a model of discipline in the area of food, I think of the dear woman who volunteered to come to our house and tutor my daughter in reading. By her physical appearance, it was obvious that this wonderful woman definitely did not have a weight problem.

Well, one morning I found out one of her "secrets." She arrived right at 10:00 A.M. (another discipline!) for the tutoring session. As I ushered her to the desk where the instruction was to take place, I also carried a crystal serving bowl mounded with beautiful, luscious bing cherries—my favorite! I had washed them, and oh, were they ever shining! Well, as I set the bowl down on the desk along with a few napkins for her and my daughter to use, this woman looked up at me, smiled graciously, and said, "Oh, no thank you. I've already had my breakfast."

The message—at least to my heart—was, "Oh, no thank you. I've already had my breakfast. In fact, I had it at the *appropriate* time. So I'm not hungry now and I don't need to eat now. It's not time to eat now. And when it is time to eat lunch, I'll eat again then, at the *appropriate* time."

Wow! A big lesson learned! (Or maybe three lessons! #1—She was on time. #2—Tutoring is business and she came to work with my daughter, not snack and socialize. #3—She ate her meals at the *appropriate* time...and didn't snack in between.)

2. *Read on self-control and life management*—Start your own reading program and keep a file of important things you learn in this all-important *spiritual* area dealing with your *physical* life.

3. *Look to God's Spirit for Christlike self-control*—Paul wrote, "But the fruit of the Spirit is...self-control" (Galatians 5:22-23). This means that when we walk by the Spirit, submitting ourselves and our passions, urges, and appetites in obedience to Him, we will not fulfill the lust of the flesh

(Galatians 5:16). Desiring to live a Christlike life and looking to the Holy Spirit for His enablement is how you and I can crucify the flesh with its passions and lusts (verse 24) and enjoy the personal discipline and temperance God calls us to.

4. *"Make no provision for the flesh"* (Romans 13:14) —Making provision points to forethought and to planning ahead. The Bible urges us not to allow thoughts of sin and of fulfilling those thoughts of sin to linger in our minds. Why? Because the longer we allow such thoughts to remain in our minds, the more provision we find ourselves making for the fulfillment of those sins.

   For instance, a simple way that you and I as home managers can make no provision for the flesh is by *not* purchasing certain items for our pantry and refrigerator. For instance, if cookies are in the house, somehow we (and the members of our household) end up eating cookies! Why? Because we made provision for the act of eating cookies. But if cookies aren't in the house, somehow we (and the members of our household) find our way to a better choice, such as a piece of fruit.

5. *Just say NO!*—Personal discipline can be as simple as the two-letter word NO! Christ didn't say, "Indulge yourself." Instead He said, "Deny yourself" (Matthew 16:24). So, just say NO! (And, as the woman who visited my house sweetly added, "No, *thank you*.")

6. *Pray*—Have you seen the number of weight reduction books that are now offered in the Christian book market? I meet women everywhere

who are having tremendous success in this ever-present, ongoing battle against the flesh. And from woman after woman I hear this one thing—the books say to *pray*—pray about food choices, pray at the beginning of each day for self-control, pray before each meal for moderation, pray with each twinge of hunger, pray in every temptation, pray at each food encounter, pray at the end of each day. Prayer, dear one, lifts our sights upward—off of ourselves, off of our earthly appetites, off of our physical desires, and assists us in seeking those things which are above...and setting our mind on things above, not on things on the earth (Colossians 3:1-2). And prayer also connects us to the grace and power of Almighty God who is able to aid those who are tempted (Hebrews 2:18). What a rich—and simple—resource! So pray!

Your Emotional Life

Oh, here's a hotbed (and another area that calls for maturing in moderation and discipline)! Stress and strain are everywhere. They're rampant! As one woman remarked, "I live on a steady diet of stress!" We have so many God-ordained responsibilities, roles, relationships, and commitments to live out! And besides that, there are a multitude of other activities that worm their way into our life—some worthy and some not so worthy.

But, as we've been learning, we must grow in our ability to manage pressure and provide a much-needed model of emotional discipline for others. Are you ready for some help toward greater emotional strength and stability?

- *Think of models*—Once again, think of the women you know, perhaps in your own church, who model the personal discipline and self-control and temperance we're learning about.

I know my mind flashes instantly to one precious woman and one particular incident that taught me volumes about emotional control, about being calm under fire. In fact, that red-letter incident helped me to turn an important corner in this area of Christian maturity.

In retrospect, it was a very small thing, but it taught me a large lesson. It happened the night of the elders' meeting at our church when, as usual, the elders' wives were serving our men a potluck dinner. With two little ones in tow, I finally arrived at the church kitchen, a little late, breathless, frazzled, and in tears. It had just been "one of those days" for me, one of those days when nothing goes the way you planned!

Well, it would have been one thing to arrive a little late and breathless and frazzled with a pan full of beautifully baked beans as my offering to our men and to the Lord. But I arrived a little late and breathless and frazzled...with a pan of dried-up, shriveled-up, *burned-up* baked beans! (Yes, my offering was burnt!) Hence the tears.

But the dear woman who comes to mind as a model of emotional stability calmly came to my rescue. First, she tenderly patted me on the shoulder and told me not to worry, that of course the beans could be used. Then, after being assured that I, a *person*, had been ministered to, she turned her attention to the awful *pan* of brown goo and said, "We'll just boil some water and pour it over the beans and mix it in. No one will be able to tell the difference. They'll be delicious!"

And then she did just that. The *beans* were revived under the wisdom and wand of her experience with such matters. *I* was helped (indeed, made into a success!). And *she* never lost her cool, calm, rational manner. She never missed a beat. She never lost her dignity (as I had). And she never put out an all-points bulletin—"Hey, everyone look what Liz did! What are we going to do?! We have no beans for the men's dinner!"

As you can tell, this incident has nothing to do with drunkenness. No, it's about beans! But it's also about the meaning of the trait we're considering. Because this woman had achieved the mature mark of moderation and discipline and quiet sobriety *in every area of her life* (including her manner and emotions), she has served as a minister to me *and* to countless other younger women in our church.

Looking back at the great baked-bean ordeal and trying to put my finger on exactly what this true-in-the-biblical-sense older woman did and how she did it (or maybe what she *didn't* do and how she *didn't* do what she *didn't* do!), here are a few of my observations.

— She remained calm throughout the crisis.
— She was able to think quickly and make a decision that saved the day (and my reputation…and the beans).
— She used discretion in choosing from among options—options like sounding the alarm, alerting others, telling me what I should do next time, judging my capabilities based on one failure.
— She had my personal good in mind and ministered directly to me and my situation.

— She went into action…calmly, and was most definitely characterized (as opposed to my falling-apart state) by reason, sanity, and self-control, showing both mental and emotional balance.

— To sum up her behavior, she was cool, collected, composed, and rational versus excited, agitated, frustrated, disturbed, irritated, and out of control. She modeled all of the wonderful definitions that describe this wonderful and important lifestyle of temperance, moderation, and personal discipline.

As I said, it was a large lesson for me, one that remains vivid these several decades later. It's also been a lesson that I've carried in my heart and mind and drawn upon in my dealings with other women who are going through their own personal rendition of my baked-bean episode.

• *Cultivate regular quiet times*—When you and I *don't* meet with the Lord regularly, we tend to forget the power and assurance we possess in Him. Our daily time in God's Word and in prayer renews the calmness and strength and perspective we experience while lingering in His presence. With that comes peace from trusting in Him and the posture of a heart at rest. Therefore, when we *do* sit faithfully before the Lord and regularly feast upon His Word, then, when we meet up with a stressful situation (or a tempting one!)...

    ...we are more likely to look to the Lord and draw upon the composure we so enjoy during our quiet times.

    ...we are more likely to remain calm, because we know what it's like to be still in the presence of God (Psalm 46:10).

...we are more likely to restrain ourselves from impulses, appetites, and desires, because we know firsthand from our time in God's Word that truly, we "shall not want" (Psalm 23:1), that the Lord, our Shepherd, will take care of all our needs as well as strengthen us in times of temptation and fully supply His all-sufficient grace (2 Corinthians 12:9).

...we will better know God's Word and want to obey it instead of seeking fleshly satisfaction. As my pastor writes, "It is only as we 'walk by the Spirit' that we 'will not carry out the desire of the flesh'....And to walk by the Spirit is to live by the Word."[2]

....we are more likely to want to heed God's higher callings than to listen to our selfish and fleshly longings.

...we are more likely to move down (and move down it more quickly!) the path of becoming one of those temperate, controlled, disciplined-in-every-aspect women who graciously floats through life and each day of it, unruffled by stress, untouched by the temptations of this world, unbothered by life's surprises and its many Plan B's...and who ministers to others like you and me who so need her model, her presence, and her ministry!

...we will become slaves of Christ (Galatians 1:10) instead of slaves to the flesh, to food

and drink, to the telephone, to mall out-
ings, to *TV Guide,* to the daily soap
operas, to romance novels. We'll be
wholly devoted to Him and to serving His
people, as other things have less and less
claim on any part of our life. As the old
familiar hymn affirms, "the things of earth
will grow strangely dim in the light of His
glory and grace."[3]

- *Work the study guide*—If you have the growth
  and study guide that accompanies this book,[4]
  please do the study. Getting into the Scriptures
  for yourself will strengthen you. As you know,
  God's Word is alive and powerful, sharper than a
  two-edged sword and helps us to discern the
  thoughts and intents of our heart (Hebrews 4:12).

  If you don't have the study guide, spend time
  looking up the many scriptures I'm sharing
  throughout these chapters in your own Bible.
  Mark them. Memorize them. And make them your
  own.

Your Practical Life

If you've read any of my books, you already know that
I'm a planner. This habit hasn't come naturally or easily for
me. No, becoming a planner is for me the result of years
and years of following through on the daily discipline of
planning each day, each week, each month, each quarter,
each year, and even each hour!

But I do want to remind you that *sober-mindedness* is our
working definition of a woman who possesses personal discipline and sobriety and a measure of control. In short, we're
talking about a woman who is calm, tranquil, serene, steady,

and staid. And I want to urge you to learn to use your *mind* to plan, to grow in the use of your *mind* until you are an expert in the area of planning.

And to get you started on your new life of planning and to assist you in enjoying the pleasant fruits of a calm, controlled, and disciplined life due to better planning, check out these two exercises.

✓ Use your mind to pinpoint any weaknesses in the physical area. Then use your mind to plan a solution in that area, to plan for victory. For instance, is your weakness cookies? Then don't purchase cookies! Is it stress build-up? Then plan for a quiet time (or two) during the day, or at least plan to remember some favorite verses that remind you of God's presence, peace, and protection. Is it weight gain? Then use a smaller plate. Eat more servings of fruits and vegetables each day. Begin walking each day. Also begin making wise, healthy substitutions for things like ice cream, whipped cream, half-and-half, and whole milk. (I'm sure you know all about this! What woman doesn't?!)

✓ Use your mind to pinpoint the times each day when things tend to fall apart. I know that these "times" have changed for me over the years, but I remember all too well as a busy wife, mom, and home manager of a full and active nest trying to walk through what I called "the tightrope times" each day. Those were the times when everyone in our family was at home. Everyone was up and on the move. Jim was getting ready for work and the girls were getting into trouble. Or, as time passed, Jim was getting ready for work and the girls were getting ready for school. I was frantically trying to get breakfast on the table and lunches into sacks, double-checking on the car pool, dealing with the dog, and getting ready myself if it was Bible study day.

Another "tightrope time" hit after school, when everyone began to find their way back home. Then, as our girls turned into young adult women with jobs, night classes, study groups, friends, and social gatherings, our pressure times moved from afternoons to late evenings.

How did planning help to better these all-too-familiar daily scenes? Well, once I thought through and analyzed my days and used my mind to pinpoint the daily pressure times, I could then put my mind to use in solving the problem. For instance, instead of working at a breakneck pace right up to the moment someone walked through the door, I could plan to stop my activities 30 minutes early. I could plan to prepare for the homecoming of my family. I could tidy the house, set out a snack, put on some quiet music. I could prepare to meet and greet and minister to them...instead of being irritated, interrupted, and surprised by their arrival. Instead of a scene in the kitchen each morning, I could double-check on the car pool the night before, and set out the sacks and the non-perishable items for lunch the night before.

When you do these exercises (and, please, do them often!), I'm sure you'll discover many wonderful practical ways to plan and improve your life and the lives of those nearest you. As you bring discipline into your practical life through planning, your home will turn into more of a "Home, Sweet Home"! And your life will turn into more of a "Life, Sweet Life"! All because of a measure of personal discipline, sober-mindedness, moderation, and self-control.

Looking Upward

Much of what I've shared in this chapter reflects my own experience and the trials and errors and struggles of my life as a woman who became a Christian after being married eight years and having two children. During those first eight years, I had no discipline, so you can be sure our lifestyle, our home life, and our children had no discipline. But over the years I've attempted to pursue a disciplined lifestyle. Why? Because in Titus 2:3 God calls me to it. And oh, did (and do) I ever want to answer my Savior's callings upon my life—each and every one of them! So I've dipped into my own experiences to try to communicate my understanding of the beauty and blessings of the hard-won, godly essential of personal discipline.

But for you, my dear reading sister, the best way to determine whether you should or should not do something—even the things I suggest and share in this book—is to sift each choice and option through the grid of Scripture. Look not to me, but to the Word of God. Look to the Lord, dear one. *He* will show you the best way to live for Him!

Essential

*"the older women [are to] be...teachers
of good things"*
—TITUS 2:3

*"We tend to think of encouragement as meaning
to build up or cheer up another person so that
they* feel better. *However, God's word for
encouragement means training, disciplining,
and helping others by helping them to be
sober-minded...so that they* live better."

*"When godly Christian women do not infuse the
younger generation with the things of God, the
church comes to dire straits."*
—JOHN MACARTHUR

*"God is calling you to be a teacher of good
things! And it's crucial to the health of the
Church that you answer His calling. And you
have so much to give—more than you think!"*

Chapter Seven

A Woman's High Calling to Encourage Others

I's been said that a holy life has a voice that speaks when the tongue is silent. Do you know a woman whose godly life speaks and teaches...even when and while her tongue is silent? And, more important than that question is this one: Are *you* becoming this kind of woman, a woman whose very life shows and encourages others how to live out God's high calling to His women?

Well, our next essential from the Lord is His assignment to you and me to be *teachers of good things* (Titus 2:3). We are to be teaching *good things* to other women—*things* that are good, virtuous, right, and noble. We are to teach others by our example and to set a high standard for them by our conduct.[1]

I know that I've been greatly blessed by God to have "grown up in the Lord" in a wonderful church, literally surrounded by dozens of the splendid "older" women Paul points us to in Titus 2:3. Yes, I know I've been blessed. But one day last week I caught a glimpse of exactly *how* blessed I am when I received a five-page letter from a woman in Ireland who has *no one* to look up to! *No one* to teach her and show her the way to godly living! *No one* to encourage her in her pursuit of God's high calling. In fact, she was so taken by my descriptions of the many older women in my church who have faithfully modeled for me and taught and mentored me in God's ways that she wanted to make her next two-week vacation one to Southern California. She wanted to actually visit my church and meet these dear women who mean so much to me!

Oh, dear precious reader, I hope you will commit your life to becoming one of these precious "older" women to anyone and everyone who is "younger" than you. I hope and pray that yours is a long, dedicated life filled with days of filling up others with all of the *good things* that you know and they yearn to know! And I hope no one ever receives a letter from someone in *your* church who says there are no older women who are "teaching good things." For, indeed, to be *teachers of good things* is God's will for your life! It's one of His high callings upon your life and an essential for godly living for you and me as His women.

So...what does it mean to be a *teacher of good things?*

A Definition

To begin with, the word translated "teachers of good things" is another of those unique words used only once in the New Testament—only here in Titus 2:3.

And it's a compound word—*kalodidaskalos. Kalos* means beautiful, good, valuable, and virtuous. The Greeks used the word "good" to refer to anything that was beautiful in form, excellence, goodness, or usefulness. And *didaskalos* means a teacher and an instructor, such as a doctor or a master. When combined, it signifies a teacher of the right, a teacher of what is excellent, a teacher of good things.

A Few Words of Explanation

We've already seen several negatives (or *bad things*) that God's women are not to be and not to do and not to model—they are *not* to gossip, and they are *not* to drink too much wine (verse 3). However, on the positive side, Christian women are to spend their time and efforts on better things, on *good things* instead. And they are to be teachers of that which is good.

And exactly where is the classroom to be, the platform for the teaching that these wonderful older women are to impart? And exactly what is to be taught...and why? Here's what we learn from Titus 2:3-5.

The Church—As we see in the book of Titus, the church is the topic of Paul's letter to the young pastor Titus. Paul is letting Titus know how to organize the church on the island of Crete. For the sake of order, Paul prescribes specific roles for each member (Titus 2:1-8). When he addresses the role of the older, more mature women in the church, he in essence says that they are to put their efforts into teaching other women. They are to be spiritual instructresses. "Although women are forbidden to teach or have authority over men (1 Timothy 2:12), they do have the God-given responsibility to formally and informally teach children, especially their own, and younger women in the church."[2] We must, therefore, my friend and sister-in-the Lord, take to heart the fact that God's Word says that one of our God-given roles is to live out God's high callings in our own life and then to teach those callings to other women in the church.

The Home—also emerges as a natural arena for the teaching of *good things*. The scriptural text specifically mentions husbands and children and the home. Paul points out that he expects the older women, rather than Titus, to be the teachers of the young women, considering it a domestic function.[3]

The Content—We'll spend more time (indeed, the rest of this book!) on the content and the curriculum that God wants these noble older women to teach. But for now, here is God's "Table of Contents" as listed in Titus 2:4-5. I think you'll find that each subject is truly an essential for godly living for us as women. The older women are to "admonish the young women" or to "encourage" (NASB) them in these areas—

- how to love their husbands
- how to love their children
- how to be sensible
- how to be pure
- how to be homemakers
- how to be kind
- how to follow their husband's leadership

The Purpose—There's a wonderful purpose behind what Paul is defining as a key role for the women in the church: The experienced older women are to live out godliness and teach a lifestyle of godliness to the younger women so that (and here's the purpose) the younger women are *encouraged*.

We tend to think of *encourage* as meaning to build up or cheer up another person so that they *feel better*. However, Paul's meaning is more serious than that. His word for *encourage* means train, discipline, and help others by—and to the point of—making them sober-minded.

Furthermore, this training actually means "to make sober-minded." And this training is done by purposeful discipline and by holding one to his duty.[4] As my pastor explains, to *encourage* literally means "to cause someone to be of sound mind and to have self-control." It is closely related to sensibleness and self-restraint. Therefore, you and I are to help other women to "cultivate good judgment and sensibilities"[5] so that they *live better*...and so that "the word of God may not be blasphemed" (Titus 2:5). Now *that's* a high calling... and with great purpose!

The Technique—God's older women can teach others and communicate regarding His high calling in two wonderful ways—by *model* and by *mouth*. Put another way, we can teach by *personal example* and by *precept*. By *walk* and by *talk*. Both *informally* and *formally*. In other words, we are to first master God's principles and precepts personally and live them out before others. Then we are to pass them on by instruction and by wise counsel.

A Few Examples from the Bible

We're so fortunate to be able to consider several examples in the Bible of women who seem to model for us the character and the role of the "older women" Paul is referring to. Let's look at their lives in action.

> *Elizabeth with Mary*—Can you imagine the sweet time of encouragement that the elderly Elizabeth and her young cousin Mary enjoyed? We meet both of these women in Luke 1. Elizabeth was the aged wife of Zacharias the priest. The physician Luke reports that Elizabeth was barren, and that she and her husband "were both well advanced in years" (verse 7). In other words, they were beyond the childbearing years. And yet, by a miracle, Elizabeth conceived a son in her old age (verse 36).

Mary's story was quite different from Elizabeth's. Instead of being old, she was young. And instead of being married, she was a virgin. And she was a young virgin who was, also by a miracle, carrying a son, "that Holy One" who was to be called "the Son of God" (verses 27 and 35).

When these two women met together in Elizabeth's home in the hill country, they shared in uplifting fellowship in the Holy Spirit (verse 39-55) as they exalted the Lord together. Elizabeth affirmed Mary's condition and position as "the mother of my Lord," and Mary "magnified" the Lord.

Luke closes this tender scene by simply reporting that Mary remained with Elizabeth for about three months (verse 56). What do you think they talked about during those three months? Obviously we don't know. The Bible is silent. But quite possibly there was a steady exchange of instruction and encouragement. Elizabeth, as an older woman—and one who was "righteous before God, walking in all the commandments and ordinances of the Lord blameless" (verse 6)—would have much to share with her young cousin. And Mary, as an unmarried and pregnant woman, most likely welcomed Elizabeth's continued support and encouragement. Surely many *good things* were shared and exchanged between this older and younger twosome.

The True Widows—First Timothy 5:2-10 paints a truly wonderful portrait of what it means to be the kind of "older woman" we are studying in this book! The apostle Paul described for Timothy, the pastor of the church at Ephesus, what type of widows the church should support financially.

After setting the criteria that they must lack family (verses 4-8), Paul detailed the many *good things* these women who were "really widows" (verse 3) should have done throughout their lives and could most definitely teach to others. They certainly model well for us the *good things* "older women" are to live out and teach to other younger women. What were the "the good things" that these women exhibited?

> They had trusted in God (verse 5).
> They had been faithful to their husband (verse 9).
> They had dedicated their lives to doing good deeds (verses 10).
> They had gained a good reputation for Christian service.
> They had lovingly cared for and/or properly raised children.
> They had proved themselves to be hospitable.
> They had served and washed the feet of God's people.
> They had cared for and assisted those in distress.
> They had devoted themselves to doing every kind of good work.

Yes, it's plain to see by this list of magnificent *good things* that these older women had definitely lived a godly life! And they had served God's people well. They had much to pass on from their life experiences, from the good things and the good works learned and accumulated over a lifetime lived for the Lord.

The Woman of Proverbs 31—God's profile of the ideal woman (Proverbs 31:10-31) shows us many *good things* and a godly woman who teaches them to us by her lifestyle. This woman's character is good, kind, chaste, and pure. And her love for her husband, children, and home is evident (indeed a list spanning 22 verses!).

Opposites—Sadly, there are also examples of women in the Bible who did *not* live a life of godliness. But we can learn from their behavior, too. We can learn what attitudes and actions to avoid. For instance,

—"The young widows" is a category of women Paul refers to. He reports in 1 Timothy 5:13 that these women were...

> idle,
> wandering about from house to house,
> gossips and busybodies,
> saying things which they ought not.

—Euodia and Syntyche were two prominent women in the Philippian church (Philippians 4:2-3) who began arguing with one another rather than assisting others.

—Miriam in the Old Testament was the sister of Moses and Aaron. Although she was a leader of the Israelite women (Exodus 15:20), she spoke out against Moses and questioned his position (Numbers 12). God's punishment was threefold:

> She was struck with leprosy.
> She was put out of the camp of her people.
> She was never mentioned again until her
>   death (Numbers 20:1).

What lessons can we quickly learn from just these three examples of women and their behavior? In short, avoid idleness, arguing, and accusing. (These are obviously not good things.) Or, stated in the positive, stay busy, agreeable, and quiet! (Now *these* behaviors are good things!)

A Few Questions

We're wrapping up what it means to be a teacher of good things. And I have to admit it's been thrilling...and challenging! I hope you agree that God has plans for your life and mine—good plans. He wants us to be "teachers of good things." So, I have a few questions for us.

> *Are you a younger woman?* We're all younger than someone, you know. So there's obviously someone out there who is older than we are who has some mighty good things to teach us. Are you looking for those "someones"? Are your eyes wide open, observing, watching, searching, and looking at, first of all, what these dear godly older feminine saints are living out right in front of you? Are you taking note of their godly behavior—both mental and written note? I personally believe in writing down what you see and learn so that it's not forgotten or lost. So that it's retrievable when *you* turn around to teach yet another woman.
>
> And are your eyes wide open, searching and looking for one of these dear godly older feminine saints to teach you? To disciple you? To mentor you? To encourage you? To "cause you to be of sound mind and to have self-control?" To help you to "cultivate good judgment and sensibilities"? To assist you in becoming sensible and

self-restrained...so that you live better and God's Word is honored? Is yours a heart that seeks and submits to godly instruction? (I'm guessing it is, or you wouldn't be reading a book titled *A Woman's High Calling!*)

Your high calling as a younger woman is to be sure that you are growing in the essentials for godly living. God's will for your life is for you to accept and heed the instruction of godly, older, spiritual instructresses.

Are you an older woman? What I said above about being younger than someone is also true of being older than someone—we're all older than someone! So...there's obviously someone out there who is younger than you are who has a need and a desire for someone older (you?) to teach them the good things of the Lord. To teach them how to live a better life.

God, dear one, is *calling*—calling *you*—to teach these precious younger sisters-in-the-Lord. Are you wondering—"Who, *me!*"? Are you cringing—"Oh no, not *me!*"? Are you squirming—"*I* could never do *that!*"? Are you shrinking—"You've got to be kidding, Lord!"?

But it's true. *God* is calling *you* to be a teacher of good things! And it's crucial to the health of the church that you answer His calling. As my pastor writes, "When godly Christian women do not infuse the younger generation with the things of God, the church comes to dire straits."[6] And you have so much to give—more than you think...as the following story relates.

> *Grandmothers*
>
> A missionary to India was asked what was most lacking in India. He gave a fascinating answer in one word—"grandmothers"! The missionary explained: "Old women play a very important part in society—how large a part one does not realize, till one witnesses a social life from which they are almost absent. Kindly grandmothers...are the natural advisers of the young...." The missionary concluded that "the older women to whom the years have brought serenity and sympathy and understanding have a part to play in the life of the Church and of the community which is peculiarly their own."[7]

You may or may not be a grandmother. But, precious friend, that is not the point! The point is that *you* have a very important part in society. *You* are the natural advisor of those younger than you. *You* have years and understanding that those years have brought along with them. *You* have a part to play in the life of the Church and of the community which is peculiarly yours.

A Final Challenge

I just expressed to my dear Jim that I had prayed that not a single woman would read this chapter who wouldn't then utter a wholehearted "Yes!" to God's high calling to be one of His teachers of good things. As I've repeatedly said, this is *God's* calling upon your life. This is *God's* will for your life. This is *God's* lifetime goal for you.

And this is what all of the godliness (Essential #1), all of the putting away of gossip and slander (Essential #2), and all of the personal discipline (Essential #3) has been leading up to—so that *you* measure up to God's high standard for His women. So that *you* can teach others what it means to be godly by your lifestyle *and* by your lips. So that *you* can model and teach others what it means to live and move and have your being in the Lord. So that *you* can encourage so many others.

I (and of course, the Lord!) want you to own this most high calling. So here's my final challenge—which I am also using as our "Looking Upward" section.

Looking Upward

✓ Be accepting—of God's calling. He is calling you (and me), and your responsibility is to respond to His calling, to look full into His wonderful face and answer Him. Oh, please! Embrace this calling to teach, to share your life, to share the good things of the Lord with others. Indeed, it is a God-given responsibility that comes with layer upon layer of blessing!

✓ Be preparing—to teach others. We'll look at a few "teacher training" principles and how-to's in our next chapter. For now, though, don't turn the page until you've made a commitment to not only own and accept this role that God has in mind for your life, but to roll up your sleeves and commit to preparing to fulfill the role.

✓ Be available—to the women in your church. Walk where they walk. Move among them. Reach out with welcoming smiles and warm, friendly greetings. Always have a word of encouragement ready for each of them and, of course, a loving hug or pat on the shoulder. Be to them what dear Elizabeth was to her young cousin Mary.

✓ Be aware—of the younger women around you. Are any of them showing up at your side regularly? Are any of them seeking your counsel more and more often? An older woman needs "younger-woman radar." Sometimes their very presence is an open invitation to take them under your wing and "teach" them.

✓ Be praying—for yourself (!) as you accept and prepare and make yourself more available and seek to become more aware of the younger women God puts in your path. You'll need to constantly look to Him for His strength, His wisdom, His discernment, His grace, and His message as you actively set out to respond to His calling to be a teacher of good things!

Essential 4

"the older women [are to] be...teachers of good things"
—TITUS 2:3

"Here are two words of advice for women who desire to be godly. First of all, encouraging younger women is one of God's high callings upon your life. And we need to heed His calling. Each of us should be teaching and encouraging someone who is younger!

"Second, you should be learning from those who are older. Through all the ages and stages of life, God lovingly surrounds us with those who have gone before us. Someone will be available to help you."

$\mathscr{C}$hapter Eight

Encouraging Others—An Essential for Godly Living

$\mathscr{I}$t saddens me to report that the number one question I'm consistently asked by women is, "Where are the older women?" From California to Maine, women who are new in the Lord, women who have young children, women who have teens, women who need a little help with their marriages (or in-laws!), women who are single, women who want to grow in the Lord are all looking for one of the biblical "older women" described in Titus 2:3-5 to assist them. But they are searching...and searching...and wondering, "Where are they?"

In their asking, they usually go on to paint a scenario of a woman who sincerely wants to grow in the Lord and in her high callings...but just can't seem to find a woman who will help her. The good news is that younger women are truly looking for disciplers and mentors! But the bad news is that they are finding that the older women are few and far between...or afraid to answer *their* calling. But...

... *Where are* the older women? I'll give a few answers to this question at the end of the chapter. For now, though, I want us to recognize that God has given you and me two assignments in the Book of Titus.

> First, we are to be *growing* in the Lord.
> Second, we are to be *showing* others
>   how to grow in the Lord.

With these two assignments from God in mind—*growing* and *showing*—I want to first address you and me. We, dear one, are called to be and should seek to be "teachers of good things" (Titus 2:3). Our role is to encourage and "admonish the young women" (verse 4). Therefore we should set a goal of being an encourager and a teacher of other Christian women. We can be sure that such a goal is a good goal and a godly goal because it's found right here in God's Word! If you've been in search of a lifetime goal or a ministry, search no more! Here is a truly good and honorable one—teach younger Christian women.

After looking first to ourselves, we'll consider the women we're called to teach and to train, as well as a few skills to serve us along the way. After all, Paul assigned the responsibility of teaching the younger women in the church to the older women in the church. That category of "older women," my reading friend, is you and me...sooner or later!

What We Must Be

Just mention teaching and many principles come immediately to my mind! As a teacher myself—from preschool through adult education—and in my home church, I've saved these sayings and quotes about teaching:

"You cannot impart what you do not possess."

"The way you teach is important, and what you teach is more important, but how you live is most important."

"A teacher teaches by what he *says*, what he *does*, and what he *is!*"

"Jesus was the greatest teacher in the world. He knew His subject; He knew His pupils; He lived what He taught."

"You can preach a better sermon with your life than with your lips."

"You teach little by what you say, but you teach most by what you are."

"Others will follow your footsteps more easily than they will follow your advice."

Are you getting the message, dear one? I'm sure you are! It's loud and clear! To teach and encourage other women to *be* what God wants them to *be* we must first of all *be* what God wants us to *be*. And God has given us ten essentials for godly living right here in Titus 2:3-5. We are to *be*...

Dignified	Lovers of our children
Not malicious gossips	Discreet
Temperate and self-controlled	Chaste
Teachers of good things	Lovers of our homes
Lovers of our husbands	Good

These are the essentials that we'll be passing on to others, my friend, for the rest of our lives, until that day when God "calls" us to Himself. This is one of our high callings—to pass these essentials for godly living on to other women. Therefore, you and I must move toward mastering these ten essentials for ourselves...before we set about to share them with others.

I remember a lady in our church who was asked to serve on the women's committee in our Sunday school class. She was thrilled! What an opportunity! However, she later withdrew her name. Why? Because her husband thought that she ought to have a meal ready for him when he came home from work each night. He told her that once she was taking care of things at home he'd love to support her in a ministry at the church. In other words, she needed to first be and do what the Bible said she needed to be and do *before* she undertook the task of teaching and leading others. She needed to minister to those at home *before* she ministered to those at the church. I tell you, I admire both the husband and the wife in this case, who worked together as a team to tackle several of God's high callings for their marriage and home.

And now I want to "call" you, to challenge you to embrace your high calling from God and to own it. To pay attention to what we're learning in this book about God's high calling to us as His women. To be diligent about following after and living out His essentials. What will this require?

What We Must Do

First of all, growth is on the top of the list! Be sure *you* are growing. Do *you* need to be discipled? Do *you* need to look for a mentor? Do *you* need to spend some quality time with one of God's older women? Are *you* on a path to learning about these ten good things, these ten essentials, from the Word of God and from other godly women? Are there gaps in *your* conduct, life, skills, and disciplines that need to be filled in with God's good, better, and best things? Are there things *you* need to learn? Books *you* need to read? Classes *you* need to attend?

We might add another question here based on my friend's story above: Are there people at home you need to take care of? Are you being and doing at home what God calls you to be and do at home?

A woman who desires to live a godly life spends her life immersed in godly things and in doing good things—even fixing meals for a husband (two of God's "good things"—love your husband and be a homemaker—Titus 2:4-5). Doing the good things we're supposed to do and being what we're supposed to be is how we become "teachers of good things" (verse 3). And that, I repeat, is one of our high callings from God.

Who We Must Teach

The Bible makes it clear that "the older women" are to be "teachers of good things—that they may admonish the young women" (Titus 2:3-4). So, first of all, we are to teach younger women. And those of us who have daughters must realize the obvious priority dictated here in the natural realm—we must first be teaching our daughters and granddaughters and other female family members. (Do you remember the elderly Elizabeth and her young cousin Mary?)

First, our daughters. Teaching and training our daughters is vitally important. It's important to our dignity as women (1 Timothy 2:11-15). It's important to our husband's reputation (1 Timothy 3:4,12). It's important to the church because the passing on of godly instruction from generation to generation is the very nature of a Christian family. And it's important to us as mothers because we multiply and perpetuate our usefulness in the future homes of our children. (What son-in-law hasn't been thankful to his mother-in-law for teaching his wife to be a godly and efficient wife?!)

I know I took the teaching and training of my two daughters *very* seriously. Of course, their spiritual training took top priority, with devotions at the kitchen table twice a day and bedtime prayers. It was so much fun for all of us to be creative and vary what we did so that our times studying God's principles and God's Word were exciting. (At least *I* thought it was fun and exciting!) And going to church and Sunday school and youth groups also received top billing. I can't tell you how thrilling it is for Jim and me to watch our daughters today...reading little Bible storybooks to the babies on their laps and bundling them up to go off to church— one in Washington and the other in New York!

And, just as my two girls came home from school each day with homework from their teachers, we had "homework" assignments. Everyone helped in the kitchen, with the tasks depending on the girls' ages. Tables were set— and cleared, meals were prepared—and served, and, as I said, everyone participated. As time went by, Katherine and Courtney progressed to the point where they could select an entire menu, gather the ingredients, and prepare and serve a meal per week. I think I can safely say that both of their husbands are glad that they were trained in these "good things" of homemaking, kindness, and personal discipline (Titus 2:5).

Of course, we worked our way through the whole list of good things Paul speaks of in Titus 2:3-5. Conduct and behavior took top billing! Gossip, too, was something we worked on (or rather, worked *out* of our lives!), learning to speak well of others instead of passing on the things heard. Self-control? Well, that's always an issue for any woman, young or old, and we struggled through learning to wait...on food, on things wanted, on...(on and on the list goes!). Both Katherine and Courtney were taught and trained to respect Jim, their father, as necessary training for loving a husband in later life. Clothing selection fit well into the category of purity, as well as cultivating godly behavior with the opposite sex. As "pastor's kids" they were often on the receiving end of kindness, which we tried to duplicate toward others.

I hope you can see by these few mentions of the essentials and "good things" on Paul's list that I considered his list God's set curriculum. And I rolled up my mothering sleeves and set about to, first of all, live out God's essentials myself, and then teach them to my two daughters.

And our sons. I dearly love the Proverbs 31 woman and the entire chapter of Proverbs 31. This God-breathed, God-painted portrait of a godly woman living out her high calling shows us a mother teaching her *son!* We are struck by her passion for her son as she declares, "What, my son? And what, son of my womb? And what, son of my vows?" (verse 2). Then we notice her in the act of teaching—"The words of King Lemuel, the utterance which his mother taught him" (verse 1).

And what did she teach this little guy? Morals and leadership principles and fitting behavior for a godly man and a future godly leader (Proverbs 31:1-9). But the lessons go on! Next we read a full-blown description of the kind of woman—a virtuous woman, a godly woman—he was to look for to marry (verses 10-31)!

A child is a child is a child! And whether that child is a daughter or a son, we as Christian mothers are to participate in teaching our children the things of the Lord (Proverbs 1:8 and 31:1). Our role as teachers of good things takes time, and you may not be able to be as involved in other activities (even at the church) as you might like. But where better could we moms put our efforts that yield any higher dividends for the cause of Christ than into the lives—and hearts—of our own precious God-given children?! To not do so would be sinful neglect!

Next, the young women. In the early church and at the time of the writing of Paul's letter to Titus, pagan women were becoming Christians. Because these young Christian women had not experienced Christian love and spiritual and practical instruction in their homes while growing up, Paul called upon the older women (in age and in the faith) to show them the ropes, so to speak. These seasoned saints were to model as well as teach the essentials to the new female converts.

Beloved, the same is true today! God is calling upon you and me to share what we know—with our own daughters (and our sons) first and also with other young women. Who are the young women in your life? Other than your daughters, if you have them, look around and see who's needing your helping hand and wise words of counsel.

> Of course, there are the little "young women," the toddlers and preschoolers. How precious! I thank God every day that He's blessed me with two such little ladies in my granddaughters!

> Then there are the primary school-age girls. Are you needed to teach these perhaps? Oh, how they love to learn about Jesus!

> And how about our preteens? Many consider this to be an awkward group and thus shy away from them. (Are they girls or are they women?) Don't you think they wonder about how their lives and bodies are changing? And don't you think they would welcome an "older" friend, a friendly older woman?

> Junior highers! They may look and act formidable...but their hearts are as sweet and needy as can be. Believe it or not, they welcome anyone who is interested in them!

> High schoolers. I find these young women have generally turned a corner in teachability and are eagerly searching for help. The days beyond high school loom over their lives as a mystery—where will they be and

what will they be doing? Will they go to college? Which college? And which major? Or will they need to get a job? What kind of job? And, of course, there is almost a daily concern with the opposite sex!

I love college-age women. They've been to school for so many years that they are easily taught. And I find them anxious to learn. They really want to know all about life...and marriage...and family...and home-making. They want to know how to act and interact with others. They freely submit themselves to instruction from an older woman.

Career-age singles? What a thrill it is to assist these women with greater spiritual growth and ministry! Indeed, their freedom opens up many doors for serving God. They just need instruction and encouragement from someone willing and able to give it.

Young marrieds and moms of young children. Now, there's a group that knows they need help! They're the ones crying out, "Where are the older women?!" I know that in my life two things humbled me like no other—marriage...and then family! Suddenly the turf was totally new. And the challenges were constant. These were new roles, each calling for new information. How I thank God (again) for the long line of older women who have assisted me in growing up!

Mothers of teens. These dear women spend most of their time praying! Will what they've faithfully poured into their children's lives take root? Will the good things imparted blossom in their children's hearts? These concerned mothers literally hang on to every word of encouragement and comfort and assurance you utter to them!

There are others—mothers with empty nests, mothers with new daughters-in-law (not to mention daughters-in-law with new mothers-in-law!), women whose husbands have left them, young widows, older wives whose husbands are suffering physical afflictions.

My point is, as we've scaled the age groups and needs of "younger" women, that whatever your age is, *someone* out there needs you to teach them, to admonish them, to encourage them! So...are your eyes open? Are your ears open? Is your heart open?

What We Must Teach

I know I've hammered away on the fact that Titus 2:3-5 *is* what we are called by God to teach to the younger women in our life and in our church. Titus 2:3-5 *is* the God-ordained curriculum.

But I do want to address one consistent element that needs to be primary and prominent in *all* of the teaching times and in *all* of our encounters with our precious younger sisters, and that is the spiritual life. The devotional life. Whenever you and I meet with another woman we must make sure that we share the things of the Lord. Why? These young women can turn to a multitude of other sources and resources for *practical* advice. But what *you* as a godly woman can offer them, in addition to the practical instruction on marriage, family, and home life, is *spiritual* instruction. As the one gentleman interpreted the term "teachers of good things," we are to be "spiritual instructresses."[1] Two particular instances stand out to me.

First, is the encounter between Elizabeth and Mary. (You may want to refresh your memory of their meeting and their time together by reading Luke 1:39-56.) The visit this older and younger woman enjoyed is described by the Bible as a spiritual time of worship. It was spiritually uplifting...and uplifting of God. Surely Elizabeth's words of acclamation and affirmation encouraged the young mother-to-be Mary. And surely the friendship of these two women was strengthened by mutual sharing centering on the Person and work of God. Worship, words of encouragement, the wonder of God, and wonderful fellowship—these are certainly some of the *good things* that should make up every older-woman/younger-woman encounter as they exchange the *good things* of the Lord.

And second, is an "encounter" one of my friends (an experienced discipler and mentor of young women) had with one of her disciples. Their meetings were initiated by the younger of the two...due to a problem. As they met, week after week, my friend was concerned that no change was taking place. The problem was still present. And no sign of inroads to victory in the situation was evident or even forthcoming!

Well, one day this true older woman asked her younger sister-in-Christ how her devotional times were going. The answer was sort of a *"What* devotional times?" answer. You see, the younger woman was depending on my friend to remedy her problem. She was reaching out to my friend for the solution. Oh, the remedy and the solution were there, and it was true to God's Word. But the *power* to put the remedy and the solution to use was missing.

So an assignment was given—to have a devotional time every day. When the younger woman passed her accountability sheet to my friend at the next meeting, sure enough, she had met with the Lord only one time that week. And so about three more weeks passed, weeks with a *weak* showing on the young-married's part in the devotional area!

I have to report to you that my friend then did a very hard thing! She told this young woman that when she had met with the Lord through time in His Word and through time in prayer for 30 days in a row she would meet with her again.

Oh, dear older woman and precious younger woman! Our calling to be God's women is a high calling. And in our teaching—and learning—of the good things of the Christian life, we must center on the God who issues forth the high callings to godly living and on His Word. The devotional life, the spiritual life, must be first and foremost. As another of my favorite teacher-quotes states, "As all roads lead to Rome, all teaching should lead to Christ."

And one more thought about my friend and this tough decision she made. She was doing exactly what the word "teach" or "train" or "encourage" or "admonish" means. It means "to make sober-minded," and it "is done by purposeful discipline and holding one to his duty." Ever wise, this older-in-the-faith-and-age woman held her younger sister accountable to the #1 essential to godly living—centering our life on God! She gave her a homework assignment...and held her to it. She *discipled* her by *disciplining* her. That's what discipleship is—helping the younger saints to grow by showing them the guidelines from God's Word...and then holding them accountable. Assisting them in living their life between the lines, so to speak.

(By the way, my friend's firm-but-loving decision worked magnificently! I wish you could meet "the younger woman" who is today a mature Christian, a loving wife, and a godly mother of four!)

Looking Upward

Do you remember that we began this chapter with a question, "Where are the older women?" Here's an answer from my heart to yours as we look upward to God's high calling and onward to mutual service.

I've given this question much thought, even to the point of examining my own life. There is no doubt that many women (estimates suggest well over 50 percent) hold down jobs, reducing the amount of time and availability they have for meeting with younger women. I also know *many* women who continue to pour their lives into their own children through home schooling and into their grown and married daughters and their grandchildren. And there are others who travel with their husbands in their later years. And, unfortunately, there are those who have not grown, who have little to give, and who spend their time on other pursuits.

So I have two words of advice for you, dear reader. First of all, remember that encouraging younger women is one of God's high callings upon your life. We need to heed His calling. Each of us should be teaching and encouraging *someone* who is younger! Whether you work outside the home or not, God is asking you to have a hands-on ministry to the younger women in your family and church. So dedicate your life to training the most obvious and natural "younger people" in your life, your own children and grandchildren. Join with God, ask for His help, and set about to see that (by His grace!) godly women are raised up and handed over to the next generation.

Second, you and I should be learning from those who are older. Through all the ages and stages of life, God lovingly surrounds us with those who have gone before us. It may take a lot of prayer and patience and active searching on your part, but don't give up. *Someone* will be available to help you.

So...here's a checklist for both older and younger:

✓ Don't give up in your search for an "older woman." There are also numerous older women who have put their wisdom in writing. Good books abound that come from the hearts and souls and minds of a multitude of older women in the faith. Also try to attend events where older

women are teaching and sharing their knowledge.

✓ Realize that *you* may be one of the older women
in your congregation. If so, don't resist. Embrace
the reality and do all you can to serve those in
your church.

✓ Be sure you are growing in the Lord. I repeat,
you cannot impart what you do not possess. Spiritual growth *now* ensures that you will always
have something vital to pass on to others.

Essential 5

"...admonish the young women to love their husbands..."
—Titus 2:4

"A wife's esteem and admiration for her husband should always be on display, on parade, so that no one can miss it. Such respect encompasses all of the things—both little and large—that she does to create a visual expression of love."

"We are to love our husband as a best friend, as someone we enjoy and enjoy being with. To spoil him. To think of him. To pray for him. To encourage him. To welcome him. To nurture a deep friendship with him."

Chapter Nine

A Woman's High Calling to Her Marriage

Are you married, dear friend? If so, pay heed to these next two chapters because they will spell out for you yet another of God's high callings for your life—that you are to *love* your husband.

Are you single? You'll find excellent information here for you as well. How can that be? Because you never know *what* (or should I say *who?*) is around the corner in your life! And you also never know what women the Lord will place in your path to minister to. It just might be a married woman who doesn't know what God's wonderful Word has to say to her about being a wife.

In our previous two chapters we learned that the older women are to be teachers of good things to the young women (Titus 2:3-4). We also looked at the curriculum God assigns us to teach to others. And #1 on His list is that you and I are to be actively admonishing and encouraging the young women "to love their husbands." (This, of course, also means that we're to be sure that we are loving our own husband!) I've marked these four words from Titus 2:4—*to love their husbands*—heavily in my Bible. Why? Because this instruction from God appears *first* on His list of things I as a married woman need to know and do. Therefore, my being God's kind of wife is obviously important to Him and should be important to me. It's one of His high callings.

And it *is* important to me! So important, in fact, that I researched the Bible to see what it teaches about my roles and responsibilities as a Christian wife. What follows is a brief sketch of what I found in the treasure of God's Word. You'll want to familiarize yourself, too, with the scriptural passages in your own Bible from which this summary is drawn—Genesis 2 and 3; 1 Corinthians 11:3-12; 2 Corinthians 11:3; and 1 Timothy 2:9-15.

Now, let's see what God has in mind for Christian wives, for indeed, being a loving wife is another essential for godly living!

The Role of a Wife

A woman once asked me, "What really happened there in the Garden of Eden?" The Garden of Eden—that's where our role as a wife was first defined! As we consider the Bible's account of the creation of mankind and a few other specific scriptures, we learn that...

A wife is to help her husband—To grasp the importance of our role as a helper, we need to understand that man was created first, by God, to have dominion over every living thing on the earth. We also learn that woman was created *after* man, *from* man, *for* the man, and for a purpose—to *help* him (Genesis 2:18).

What does this mean? It means that man needed a companion, a helper, someone to complete him. And, if you are married, that *someone* is you. God's high calling to you is to help your husband with *his* responsibilities, *his* tasks, *his* roles, *his* work, and *his* callings from God.

A wife is to follow her husband—We can be sure that God's creation was glorious! Imagine the perfect environment—the Garden of Eden—with its perfect beauty! Then add a perfect husband and a perfect wife to that image.

Unfortunately, however, the Fall followed the Creation. The serpent entered paradise and tempted the woman...who gave in to the temptation...who then tempted her husband...who then gave in to the temptation. As God dealt with all parties, He made it clear that the man was to lead and the woman was to follow (Genesis 3). These assignments are also repeated in the New Testament, letting us know several more times that the husband is to lovingly lead and the wife is to submit herself to his leadership and follow him (Ephesians 5:22-32; Colossians 3:18-19; 1 Peter 3:1).

And what does it mean to follow? Again, our understanding becomes clearer when we learn that #1) "submission" or "subjection" is a military term portraying the voluntary lining up of one person under the authority of another, to willingly rank oneself under another;[1] and #2) "submission" is a choice and a decision that wives must make—to choose to submit *themselves* to the leadership of their own husband.

We learn in Titus 2:5 how important our submission and obedience and following of our husband is: Paul wrote to Titus that the wives were "to be...obedient to their own husbands, that the word of God may not be blasphemed." Paul is asking that we wives willingly submit to our husbands, not only because it is God's will for us, but also because God's Word would be ridiculed if the watching world were to see a disobedient wife. In other words, when we fail to follow our husband, the word of God is dishonored.

A wife is to respect her husband—We've learned that we are to *help* our husband and we are to *follow* our husband. And now, according to Ephesians 5:33, we are also to *respect* our husband.

And what does this mean? To respect a husband means actively demonstrating and showing high regard for him in ways that all can see. A wife's esteem and admiration for her husband should always be on display, on parade, so that no one can miss it. Such respect encompasses all of the things—both little and large—that she does to create a visual expression of love.

A wife is to love her husband—And now we come to the text for this chapter, which is another of God's high callings to you and me as wives and another essential for godly living for us as married women—we are to *love* our husband (Titus 2:4). Evidently in the early church marital problems arose as marriages were pre-arranged by parents, as married women came to Christ and their husbands didn't, and as women were many times considered only a means of producing heirs. Paul therefore wrote—often and in many of his letters—to exhort wives who were Christians to "change their attitudes and actions toward both their saved and unsaved husbands."[2]

The Love of a Wife

Have you heard sayings like these about "love"?

Love makes the world go 'round.

True love doesn't consist of holding hands— it consists of holding hearts.

Love is more easily demonstrated than defined.

Love is the fairest flower that blooms in God's
garden.

Love is something different from delirium, but it's
hard to tell the difference.

True love doesn't have a happy ending; true love
doesn't *have* an ending!

While we might think these quips and quotes are sweet
or cute, we as Christian wives need to know more—we
need to know what the Bible means when it calls us to love
our husband.

A definition—First of all, God's summons to love in Titus
2:4 is not referring to romantic love. And it's not about sexual
love. No, "to love your husband" is a reference to *friendship*
love, and occurs only here in the New Testament. The
phrase comes from the Greek word *philandros* and refers to
"willing, determined love that is not based on a husband's
worthiness but on God's command, and that is extended by
a wife's affectionate and obedient heart."[3] This "*phileo* love,
often used to describe the 'emotional' dimensions of love,
involves 'friendship.' It expresses 'delight' in doing something. It refers to doing something with 'pleasure.'"[4]

And, dear fellow wife, we are to *show* it. This is the kind
of love we *show* to a friend. It's obvious. It's witnessed. It's
observed. It's demonstrated by what we do for our husband.
And it's communicated out of a heart of love by how we act
toward our husband. Our love is seen in the manner in
which we take care *of* him. In the way we speak *to* him. In
the way we speak *about* him. In the things we do *for* him.

A decision—Just like our decision to willingly and wholeheartedly submit to our husband's leadership and our decision to follow him, "love," too, is a decision. It's a regular

and daily choice that the wise wife makes. And then, because of her repeatedly choosing to be a loving and devoted wife, her devotion grows into a friendship that is solid and lasting and deeply ingrained to the core.

Who is your best friend? I well remember my daughter Katherine asking me one day who my best friend was. As a young, sweet, preteen wrapped up in her relationships with her best girl friends, Katherine was a little surprised when I told her that Jim, my husband and her dad, was my best friend.

And that's God's high calling to His married women. We are to love our husband as a best friend, as someone we enjoy and enjoy being with. To spoil him. To think of him. To pray for him. To encourage him. To welcome him. To nurture a deep friendship with him.

God's calling "calls" us to make a decision—will we or won't we love our husband?

An evaluation—Is the "love" missing in your marriage relationship? If your answer is Yes, then take the advice of the two scholars quoted above: Determine to act in ways that will nurture and restore your love. You and I must (and can!) train ourselves to love our husbands. And I find that's usually done by care and caring. You see, where your treasure is, there will your heart be also.

Let me explain. *Where your treasure is, there will your heart be also* is a principle spoken by our Lord Jesus in Matthew 6:21. He used it in relationship to worldly goods, citing that it is better to lay up treasure in heaven rather than on earth. I've personally found that the principle also works when it comes to time—where you put the treasure of your *time*, there will your heart be also. The same is true with care—where you put the treasure of your *care* and your efforts, there will your heart be also.

Now, dear wife, this same principle applies to you in relation to your husband. The more time and effort and care you put into loving him—serving him, cooking for him (his favorites, of course!), taking care of his laundry, pressing his shirts and slacks, folding his clothes and putting them into his drawers (that you are also making sure are neat and orderly!), the more love you will find growing in your heart.

Every thoughtful deed and every kind thought toward your mate is evidence of your loving concern. Every menu planned and meal cooked with him in mind, every chore performed that betters his life and the place where he lives, every tender word of praise and affirmation spoken, every tiny touch, every prayer lifted to God on his behalf, and every sweet smile that graces his life from your lips shouts of your love!

And, as you make a point of pursuing such deeds of love, in time you will find your heart changing. You see, you've invested too much time and labor in bettering his life to not care about him. Even when a response from him is not forthcoming or is not quite as fantastic as you might wish, a spirit of love is blossoming in *you!* Plus your loving care is made strikingly clear to your cherished husband and is witnessed by all—by your precious husband and by anyone who happens to be nearby! Indeed, it can't be missed!

The Tales of Two Wives

As I was turning the pages of my Bible and looking at the marriages of couples portrayed in God's Word, I found one wife who most definitely did *not* live out God's directives to love and help and submit to and respect her husband, and one who did.

First the positive—the Shulamite. Song of Solomon is the beautiful book of the Bible that details the courtship, marriage, and maturing relationship between King Solomon and a Shulamite woman. At some point in their marriage, the question was asked of the Shulamite, "What kind of beloved is your beloved?" (Song of Solomon 5:9, NASB). The wife then began to praise her husband to others. Listen as she speaks: "My beloved is white and ruddy, chief among ten thousand....His mouth is most sweet, yes, he is altogether lovely. This is my beloved, and this is my friend...." (verses 10 and 16).

Later, this woman who so clearly loved her husband spoke these words to her mate: "I am my beloved's, and his desire is toward me. Come, my beloved, let us go forth to the field; let us lodge in the villages. Let us get up early to the vineyards; let us see if the vine has budded, whether the grape blossoms are open, and the pomegranates are in bloom. There I will give you my love" (Song of Solomon 7:10-12). Can't you just picture the love and respect this woman had for her husband, her beloved, and her friend? She desired to be with him, to love him, to please him...and she delighted in praising him.

Next the negative—Michal. King David was truly a man after God's own heart (Acts 13:22). In fact, he loved God so much that when the ark of the Lord was finally returned to Jerusalem, he expressed his love and emotion for God by dancing and praising Him as the ark was carried into the city. David ordered that sacrifices be made to God and that a great celebration take place.

But when David's wife Michal watched David at worship, the Bible reports, "she despised him in her heart" (2 Samuel 6:16). Her heart of contempt then overflowed with bitter words and resentment as she met David at the door with words of disgust to this effect: "Your actions were undignified! Your appearance was unworthy! You looked and acted like a fool! You behaved basely and shamefully!" Michal failed to demonstrate love and respect for her husband. She allowed contempt to overcome her. Her words were expressions of deep-seated hatred, disdain, and bitterness. And her heart was obviously a storehouse of hatred, for as our Lord Jesus said, "...out of the abundance of the heart the mouth speaks. A good man out of the good treasure of his heart brings forth good things, and an evil man out of the evil treasure brings forth evil things" (Matthew 12:34-35).

Now, my dear reading friend, pause a moment. Are you the positive wife, like the Shulamite who enjoyed spending time with her husband, being in his presence, going for walks, talking with him, complimenting him, and being his friend (Song of Solomon 5:16)? Or does the way you treat your husband and talk to him mirror the mouth and the heart of Michal—a mouth filled with insults, criticism, and put-downs and a heart fueled by disdain, a critical spirit, and contempt? Look into *your* heart and into *your* life and into *your* marriage (and at *your* words!).

A Word of Encouragement

We'll look at some practical "teaching of good things" in our next chapter on how to love our husband, but for now, set these few practices into motion. And the sooner the better!

- *Pray*—Make a decision to pray for your husband every day. How blessed I was just last evening to hear a woman share with me about how a prayer principle I've written about had helped her in her relationship with her husband. The principle is, "You cannot *hate* the person you are praying for."[5] She said something to the effect of, "Boy, did I have a tough problem on my hands! My husband and I just could not get along! But I started to pray for him every day. Was I ever surprised when God worked in *my* heart! The results and changes were so dramatic that I kept on praying...and now my hubby and I are best friends!"

Another prayer principle that's helped me tremendously as a wife who desires to shower my precious husband with every possible kind of love is related to the one above—"You cannot *neglect* the person you are praying for." I don't think many wives get up in the morning and coldly and calculatingly decide, "I think I'll neglect my husband today." No, neglect is born out of a failure to even *think* about our husband *at all!* Therefore, whenever we've completely omitted the consideration of our mate, we completely forget to do the many little things that are so important for expressing our love and building a friendship.

• *Praise*—Make a decision to praise your husband every day. Open your eyes, dear wife! Look around and take note of the countless things that your husband is doing right under your nose that are praiseworthy. For you to praise him, you've got to, first of all, notice him and his good deeds. They *are* there. And to detect them, again, you've got to open your eyes (and your heart!). You may have to hunt for his commendable acts. And you may have to look around a little (or a lot!), to search high and low, maybe even turn over a few rocks. But you must search his life each day and find something noble...and then you must verbalize your praise to him. To do so will require putting away disdain and criticism. And to put away these love-hindering attitudes will also require loving him with a large heart, seeing him through eyes of love, and lauding him with your lips.

- *Pamper*—Make a decision to pamper your husband every day (indeed, every minute!). I once heard that author and super-homemaker Emilie Barnes prepares and brings in a tea tray each evening to "her Bob." They then pause and share a cup of tea or hot chocolate together. (And if it's Emilie Barnes, you can be sure the tea tray arrives with all of the little touches she is so famous for!) One way my daughter Courtney pampers "her Paul" is by keeping balls of homemade chocolate chip cookie dough in her freezer so that she can treat him to warm cookies and milk each evening when he's home. (And, as a Navy submariner, he's gone from home 90 days at a time!)

Granted, these are little things—but they are little things that deliver a *loud* and a *large* message! I encourage you to pray for your husband, to purpose to praise him, and to "count the ways" you can pamper him. And again, the sooner the better!

A Word of Warning

How does what you're reading sound so far? I want to remind you again that God's Word is calling you and me to this most high calling to love our dear husbands. And please, don't listen to the world! You've been saved through faith in Christ Jesus. He has redeemed you and bought you out of the world. And He calls you and me as His children to put away old sinful and selfish ways and to put on new behaviors that are Christlike and selfless. Be sure you are listening to the Word of God through the Bible and to other godly people as they teach you "good things" about loving your husband.

Let's heed the word of warning these insightful thoughts convey:

Who's on First?

Why did Paul stress that young Christian women should love their husbands and families? While such teaching may appear too obvious for mention, there are forces at work in today's world that undermine even that very basic part of family life. Women are being told that their interests or desires come first, that they must seek what makes them happy before they can be good wives and mothers. While women should be encouraged to use their gifts and abilities, each Christian woman must align her priorities with God's wisdom, not the world's values. She must love her husband and her children, accepting the sacrifices that love brings. God will honor those who value what He values.[6]

Looking Upward

Do you want to "value what God values," dear one? If you've stuck with this book about God's many and glorious (and stretching!) callings upon your life this far, you are probably one of God's precious women who *does* value what He values. And, as we've been learning, heeding His calling to love our husband requires discipline, dedication, and self-denial. But, oh, the end product! Imagine a long life filled with honoring our Lord by pouring out His love to another, to a partner-for-life. And, as we've repeatedly noted, there may not ever be an overt response. There may never be any fireworks. But through the consistent choice to shower another with God's sacrificial love, *we* change! *We* grow! *We* take on the character and heart of God. *We* are transformed into the image of Christ who demonstrated and showed forth His love for us while we were yet sinners (Romans 5:8). You and I grow in godliness, in God-likeness, when we do the same for another.

So, what will it take for you and me to answer God's high calling "to love our husband" (Titus 2:4)? It will require...

Looking up to His Word...

> Titus 2:4 calls us to such love.

Looking up to His ways...

> Christ demonstrated His love for us.

Looking up to His wisdom...

> Obedience to God's Word makes even the simple wise.

Looking up to His grace...

> God's grace is always available... and always sufficient.

Looking up to His older women...

> Learn from those who love their husband.

Looking up to His calling...

> Shouldn't we desire to do and be what God desires us to do and be?

Essential 5

*"...admonish the young women to love
their husbands..."*
—TITUS 2:4

*"A choice to love your husband is a choice to
love God by obeying His high calling. And a
choice to love your husband is also a choice that
honors the Lord and is a testimony to His glory.
When we choose to love our husband, we become
'a good advertisement for the Christian faith.'"*

*"She does him good and not evil all
the days of her life."*
—PROVERBS 31:12

*"The greatest gift you can give your husband
is the gift of lifting his name and his needs before
the throne of God. Prayer for your husband
releases the energies of God, for prayer is asking
God to do what you cannot do."*

Chapter Ten

Loving Your Husband—
An Essential for
Godly Living

*J*im and I have been blessed during the 25-plus years of his ministry to know many couples at our church who truly love each other. These couples—over the long haul and into their retirement years—continue to cherish one another. How do I know that? You can see it in their eyes. You can hear it in their voices. You can tell it by the words they use when speaking to and of the other. You know it by the warm and easy feeling you have when you are with them, an all-is-well feeling. You can witness it in their many shared activities, concerns, and pursuits. Yes, you easily recognize the fact that they are friends—best friends. And you and I both know that such a relationship doesn't come without effort and determination!

This, dear reader, is what God has in mind when He asks us to make sure that we are "husband-lovers"—that we would grow in love with our husband until we become best friends with him. And, as you remember from our previous chapter, the older women are to teach and train the young women "to love their husbands" (Titus 2:4). We also noted that God calls us to a *phileo* love in the case of our husbands—that is, to an emotional, affectionate, friendship love. The goal is for Christian women who are married to learn to enjoy their husband, to like their husband, to be devoted to their husband, and to lavish love on their husband. As one scholarly gentleman stated it, women who become Christians must "get accustomed to a whole new set of priorities and privileges." He also noted that "those who had unsaved husbands would need special encouragement,"[1] creating a much-needed ministry for the older women in the body of Christ to assist them in answering this high calling from God.

Becoming Best Friends

Do you have a best girl friend or two, or perhaps a sister who fits the category of best friend? You probably do. And can you think of the many things you do for and with a best friend? Your list is probably like mine—you pray for her, phone her, send her cards and notes in the mail, celebrate her birthday, get together for lunch, visit often, email (even daily), pick up little things—little gifts whenever you're out and see something she would like. On and on the list of little things you do for a best friend goes. You spend a great deal of time and thought and even some money letting her know how special she is to you.

Well, this, my friend, is the kind of love God wants us (if we're married) to display and dispense to our husband…and even to a deeper and more devoted level than for a best girl friend. You see, "loving your husband" is *first* on God's list of assignments for us in Titus 2:3-5 as His women following His recipe for character in verse 3. Indeed, loving our husband is a high calling! So, let's see how many ways we can do the work of love and set about to answer God's calling to this essential for godly living for us as Christian wives.

Saying "I Love You"

Elizabeth Barrett Browning penned these now-famous words to her dear husband Robert—"How do I love thee? Let me count the ways." Well, not to be outdone by Mrs. Browning, I want us to brainstorm and determine how many ways you and I can express love to our husband.

1. *Make the choice to love your husband*—That's right—*decide* to love him. A choice to love your husband is most definitely a choice that will benefit both him and you. A choice to love your husband is also a choice to love God by obeying His high calling in Titus 2:4. And a choice to love your husband is also a choice that honors the Lord and is a testimony to His glory. As verse 5 teaches, we heed His callings so that "the word of God may not be blasphemed," so that the word of God will "not be discredited" (RSV). When we choose to love our husband and be obedient to him (also verse 5), we become "a good advertisement for the Christian faith."[2]

2. *Make a choice to love your husband before or ahead of your children*—I hope this doesn't sound too strange! This is not a choice to love your husband and *not* love your children. No, this is a setting of priorities. God's next high calling (which we'll get to in the following two chapters) is to love our children. But please note the order of His callings in verse 4—*before* He calls us to love our children, He calls us to love our husband. In most

cases, marriage and establishing a relationship with a husband precedes bearing children and beginning a family. And, as I once heard a wise person explain, "You live the first 20 years of your life as a single, the second 20 years as a married woman raising children, and the third 20 years with your husband." Let's see now...that's 20 years alone, 20 years raising children, and *40-plus years* as a wife. Surely the mathematics show us vividly the investment we must make in our marriage day after day!

So be careful—and be wise. When the children arrive—accompanied by all the busyness and activity that children generate—make sure loving your husband doesn't get crowded out! As I continually minister to young wives and moms, this is the chief challenge they face. (And I remember it well myself!) Your friendship and love relationship with your husband must be faithfully and diligently nurtured...even in the midst of the duties and chaos of child-raising!

3. *Submit yourself to be "taught" to love your husband*—The role of the older women in the body of Christ is to teach the young women the necessity of loving their husbands and the "how-to's" of such love. The role of the younger women is to listen and readily obey the teaching and instruction of the godly and older wise women.

I personally think this is encouraging information! Why? Because obviously such love *can* be learned. Also, it *must* be learned. And the love for a husband *can* be taught. Indeed, the older women are called upon to *teach* it. Therefore, because the fine art of loving a mate can be learned, we are not without hope!

4. *Set up a prayer book or prayer page for your husband*—Then commit yourself to pray daily for him. What should you pray for? His job. His boss. His projects and presentations at work. His challenges on the job. His appointments. His clients and customers. His role as a provider, husband, father, stepfather, and grandfather. His leadership of the family. His management of the family finances. His health. His friendships. His purity. His relationships with both sets of parents. His role as a brother and brother-in-law. His influence on any children from a previous marriage. His involvement at church. His spiritual growth and giftedness.

   Make your own list. Then make a page for each concern and category in your prayer book or prayer journal...and get to praying! The greatest gift you can give your husband is the gift of lifting his name and his needs before the throne of God. Prayer for your husband releases the energies of God, for prayer is asking God to do what you cannot do.

5. *Write a letter to God*—expressing your desire to be a wife who majors on loving her husband...no matter what kind of husband he is. As my pastor writes, "Even unlovable, uncaring, unfaithful, and ungrateful husbands are to be loved."[3]

6. *Cultivate willful love*—God's Word calls us as wives to "the duty of love." Our "first duty is to make home life attractive and beautiful by love of husband and children."[4] Indeed, such willful love is our first calling and our first duty.

   Therefore, we must listen to God's Word— not to our "feelings." As one definition of love explains, "love is…a feeling of the *mind* as much as of the heart; it concerns the *will* as much as the emotions. It describes the deliberate effort—which we can make only with the help of God…" (emphases added).[5] One teacher and interpreter of the Bible put it this way—God's "first command [for the young women] is simple and unambiguous: Young women…are to love their husbands. There are no conditions or exceptions. It is not simply that love of husbands is a virtue but that not loving them is a sin."[6] Still another Bible professor says, "Actions take precedence over feelings….To be able to [act] is a reflection of our maturity level."[7] (I'm sure you're getting the strong message this passage of scripture is sending to you and me about the need to cultivate willful love!)

7. *Listen to God's Word, not the world*—In Paul's day women were coming to faith in Jesus Christ out of pagan religions. They sorely needed the godly teaching and example of older women in both the spiritual and practical things of God. And the same is still true today. Women coming to Christ need help in putting off the teachings and standards of the world and putting on the behaviors the Word of God teaches instead. My pastor points out that today "a new generation of young women has been brought up in a society, including an education system and media, that touts feminism and belittles biblical standards for men and women. In many cases, young women even in evangelical churches have not had the benefit of careful 'teaching [of] what is good' (Titus 2:3) or the godly example of older women in the church, including that of their own mothers. Nor have they

been exposed to the clear teaching of Scripture in Sunday school, in youth group, or from the pulpit."[8] Therefore, the older, more seasoned female saints play a vital role in the training and encouragement of new converts to heed God's Word instead of the world.

Pardon me...but I'm having a quick thought or two about several real ways to keep from listening to the world:

✓ Don't read the women's magazines on the newsstands or checkout counters. (Or if you do, read with discernment!) Usually one glance at the touted contents on the covers will tell you they are filled with worldly wisdom—not godly wisdom.

✓ Beware of women's talk shows. Again, about five minutes of any one of these programs will communicate that you are getting a dose of the world's view of your role as a woman.

✓ Stay in God's Word. Your best choice of input is always the Bible. Read it. Relish it. Rely on it. And let it rule your life.

8. *Read daily on marriage*—As a new Christian and a young wife, I was a regular customer at my church bookstore and library, always browsing in the women's section and always looking for good books on being a better wife. Whenever I spotted any book on marriage, I would first see if our library had a copy of the book. My practice (in what I call our "poverty days") was to read the library copy or a friend's copy first in order to determine whether this book was one that I

wanted (or needed, as the case so often was!) to buy. If it was a "must-own" book, then the pennies were saved and the book was finally purchased. And believe me, at that moment the book became a treasure! I still own these carefully selected books and have typed out notes from them that are inches-of-typing-paper high!

And speaking of older women teaching the younger ones, whenever I disciple or mentor a married woman, I give her an accountability sheet with the days of the week (Monday through Sunday) worked into a grid. A part of her weekly assignment is to read five minutes every day on the marriage book of her choice and check it off on the grid. I found out firsthand that the simple act of reading just five minutes a day on marriage keeps me and the ladies I meet with sharp, keeps us thinking, keeps us on our toes in this vital area of nurturing a happy and successful home life. Are you unable to meet with an older woman, or unable to find one who's available at the moment? Don't despair. And don't fail to grow! Just get your own stack of books on marriage and behold what their valuable information can do to transform a marriage (as you apply their godly principles, of course!).

9. *Do the works of love heartily*—The Bible not only tells us to love our husbands, but it tells us *how* and *to what degree* and *why*— "And whatever you do [including loving your husband!], do it heartily, as to the Lord and not to man" (Colossians 3:23). In other words, love and serve him *heartily*— with hard work and a cheerful attitude. Lovingly serve him as though you were serving *the Lord Himself*. Do you think in these kinds of terms,

dear reading sister, when you're serving your husband?! This biblical mind-set truly catapults loving our husband to a completely different plane—a higher plane...a heavenly plane!

10. *Do all to the glory of God*—Here's another precept from the Bible that puts a heavenly spin to our love of husband—"Therefore, whether you eat or drink, or whatever you do [including loving your husband!], do all to the glory of God" (1 Corinthians 10:31). Now here's a high calling...that God would so permeate our lives that all we do would be to His glory! We asked ourselves questions like these earlier, but this time let's apply them to our love for our husband—"Is the service I am rendering to my husband glorifying God?" As you seek to serve your precious spouse, do you pray first and ask, "How can I glorify God through this menial service to my mate?" As Titus 2:5 teaches us, God is glorified and His Word is honored when we love our husband and are obedient to him."

11. *Confess any bitterness of heart*—Is this advice ever important! As the Bible puts it, "look...diligently lest anyone fall short of the grace of God; lest any *root of bitterness* springing up cause trouble, and by this many become defiled" (Hebrews 12:15, emphasis added). If you've been thinking as you read these two chapters about God's high calling to you to be a loving wife, "...but...I don't even *like* my husband, let alone *love* him!" then spend time as soon as possible with God in prayer, in confession, in repentance, and in supplication for yourself. Please, oh please, don't let any bitter thought or attitude take

root in your heart and home. Beware of any little thought or attitude that might grow into a great tree that would overshadow and spoil the exciting, fulfilling relationship God means for you to have with your husband. Don't become like Michal in the previous chapter who allowed a seed of bitterness to take root in her heart against her husband David, a bitterness that grew into full-blown contempt and disdain, dislike and disrespect. As the little poem *The Five "Watches"* warns us,

> Watch your thoughts—they become words.
> Watch your words—they become actions.
> Watch your actions—they become habits.
> Watch your habits—they become character.
> Watch your character—it becomes your destiny.[9]

12. *Learn to ask your husband*—"Little" things can say a lot. And I love it when a woman says a little thing like "I'll have to ask my husband." For years I've been teaching wives to say and do this one little thing—to ask their husband before they commit themselves, him, or the family to something. Why? Because a little thing like asking shows consideration for our husband. It shows a willingness to cultivate and defer to our husband's leadership. It keeps you out of trouble! Plus it teaches other wives to do the same little thing.

And now—would you believe it?—I'm on the other end of such statements! Now, whenever I try to make plans with my daughters for the holidays or ask them about a get-together or a family time, I hear from their mouths the very same words they've heard from mine over the years—"Let me talk to Paul" (each is married to a Paul!) "and call you back." "Let me see what Paul thinks…or has to say…or wants to do." "Let me see what Paul's plans are for today." "I'll have to ask Paul." Like I said, it's a little thing, but it speaks volumes! And I, for one, am thrilled and pleased and proud of my daughters each time I hear it.

13. *Put your husband first, even ahead of yourself*—
Not only is your precious spouse to be ahead of your children in priority, but he is also to be ahead of yourself. A favorite verse of mine expresses this principle this way—"Let nothing be done through selfish ambition or conceit, but in lowliness of mind let each esteem others better than himself. Let each of you look out not only for his own interests, but also for the interests of others" (Philippians 2:3-4). Our selfless service, our dying to self, and our many seeming sacrifices reap benefits and blessings for others…and for ourselves…as we do something that's important to *God* and put our husband first, even ahead of ourself!

Of course, this list of a dozen or so "ways" I've outlined is not complete—nor should it ever be complete. Love is an ever-growing and ever-deepening affection. Therefore, the works of love are unending.

Looking Upward

Maybe we should call this section "Looking Upward…and Onward…and Around." Why? Because, my precious reading friend, if you are married, I want you to do something with what we've just learned in these two chapters about being a loving wife. I want you to answer God's high calling to *you*! We must move on and act on this information from God's Word about an essential for godly living that's important to Him. So…

Are you a new Christian? Open your eyes and look around. Spot an older woman who's been a Christian for a while and watch how she loves her husband, how she helps him with his responsibilities of work, family, and church, how she follows his leadership, how she actively shows and demonstrates her respect for him.

Then go one step further—ask this older woman if the two of you could talk. It doesn't matter where (let her determine the place). And remember, you're not asking for a long-term commitment to a mentoring or discipleship relationship. Your meeting may work its way into that, but just ask to get together once. Then prepare yourself for the meeting. Arrive with a set of questions and a Bible, a journal or notepad, and a pen. Share your questions with her, and then allow this wonderful woman to share her insights with you. And don't forget to write down what she says. You certainly don't want to waste her time or her wisdom. Keep a permanent record of her counsel. Perhaps God will give *you* the opportunity to pass it on to another struggling wife.

Are you an older Christian? I hope you are seeking to live out your marriage and your life in such a way that your example motivates and instructs others in their role as a wife. A large part of the instruction in Titus 2:3-5 is about the conduct and behavior of the older women. Paul assumes that those who are older and older in the Lord are living their life in a godly manner, are not gossips, not intemperate, and are seeking to teach their younger sisters the good things of the Christian life (verse 3)—good things like how to love a husband (verse 4).

Have you learned a few lessons the hard way, or from other godly women? Have you discovered a few things that work, that help you to live out your wifely role as described in the Bible? Then, by all means, share those principles! Share the scriptures that help you to live out God's high calling to love your husband. Pass on the good news, the practical advice, the tips and the "how-to's" that make for a more successful marriage. And let me add...and ask...

Are you a mother (or mother-in-law)? Never underestimate the many lessons your attitude and actions toward your husband are teaching those closest to you! Indeed, the family is the first and best place to teach those younger women who hold first and best place in your heart—your daughters and daughters-in-law—about God's kind of husband-love. And especially enumerate the many blessings that come from putting God's Word to work in your marriage.

And speaking of blessings, I hope you enjoy the alphabet of love that follows—"Twenty-six Ways to Be His Valentine." It just happens to be Valentine's Day as I write this. And more than appreciating this wonderful author's cleverness with the ABCs, I pray you'll dedicate the rest of your life to loving *your* precious husband. May what was written of the Proverbs 31 woman be said of you—

> *She does him good and not evil*
> *all the days of her life.*

Twenty-six Ways to Be His Valentine

How long has it been since you've done something special to show your husband you love him? Here are some ideas as simple as ABC.

A morous words are not outdated. Write your husband a poem, sing him a song, buy him a romantic card.

B ake his favorite dessert and serve it by candlelight after the children are in bed.

C ompliment him—on his looks, his dedication to the Lord, his way with your children.

D rive the next time the two of you go somewhere, and let him relax and enjoy the scenery.

E numerate his fine qualities, using this modified line of Elizabeth Barrett Browning's: "Why do I love thee? Let me count the whys." Tape the list to his mirror.

F ish, golf, hunt, swim with him—or at least read up on his hobby.

G rass need mowing? Letters waiting to be typed? Give him the gift of time: do a job usually his.

H ide encouraging scripture verses or personal notes in his coat pocket, his wallet, his sock drawer, or on the pulpit.

I ndulge him with the luxury of breakfast in bed—served on a decorated tray.

J oin him for a day at his work—in his office, classroom, parishioner visitation.

K iss him goodbye when he leaves for work. It's easy to get out of the habit in the rush of life.

L earn more about him. Do you know his favorite childhood memory? The best Christmas present he ever received? His favorite music? The time he was the most afraid?

M eet him for lunch. Use fast-food coupons. Or pack a sack lunch to share.

N ew photos of the two of you can make the ordinary a day to remember. So get out the camera and frame the results.

O ld, cherished wedding pictures can help you remember when your love was new.

P repare his favorite meal.

Q uips and cartoons can lighten his day. Cut them out and give them to him on a day he needs a lift.

R ead a book together. Ralph Waldo Emerson said, "It is a tie between men to have read the same book."

S mile when you see him.

T hank him for the routine things you tend to expect him to do.

U phold him in prayer.

V alentines aren't just for February. Give him a little gift—a pen, a magazine he likes, a favorite candy bar—along with a love note.

W ash and wax the car for him.

X ercise to keep yourself looking good.

Y es, let's do it! Make that your answer when he suggests things to do—a walk, watching the sunset, taking a day to ski, whatever.

Z zzzz. Let him take a long undisturbed nap while you entertain the children elsewhere.[10]

ssential

"...admonish the young women to love
their...children..."
—TITUS 2:4

"What is a godly mother? A godly mother is
one who loves the Lord her God with all her
heart, soul, mind, and strength and then
passionately, consistently, and unrelentingly
teaches her child to do the same."

"No one has more potential for godly
influence on a child than that child's God-
fearing mother. We, therefore, are to take up the
cause, answer God's call, muster up our
courage, and set out to be the best, most faithful
teacher of God's Word and God's ways we can
be to our precious children."

Chapter Eleven

A Woman's High Calling to Her Family

*P*ardon me for chuckling as I write. But my mind is reflecting back...back to a day not too many weeks ago. Jim and I were visiting our daughter Courtney in her home in Washington. Her Paul had just left on his first-ever submarine tour...for 90 days! Jim and I had gone up to Washington from our home in Los Angeles to sort of ease the shock and help fill the void such an assignment from the U.S. Navy was bound to create.

All was going well—in fact, better than any of us had anticipated. The children were (of course!) little angels. We were all having so much fun. Being a part of their day-in, day-out lives and routines and activities was exhilarating—not to mention rejuvenating! It was such a joy to share breakfast, lunch, and dinner with the little darlings—Jacob almost two and Katie almost one. And I always delight in helping with the meals and making my gift to Courtney that of cleaning up. My standard line, is, "No, you made the meal. I can clean it up. You just go in and sit down. I don't even want you to clear the table." Honestly, after six years of an empty nest and having only Jim to fuss over, it is sheer joy to be in an active, lively home where there is actually something to clean up!

Anyway, one particular morning, Jim and I decided to run some errands (a Costco run, I think) to bring some things home for all of us. We told Courtney not to hold lunch for us, but to just go right ahead and we would see her when we got back. And off we went. As I said, all was well.

Well, we came back to Courtney's house at about 2:00. Courtney had given us a key, in case the children were into their nap time, so we let ourselves in and headed up the half flight of stairs that lead to her living room, turned the corner, and there she was (or should I say there *it* was?!). Courtney was sitting in her rocking chair with her feet up on an ottoman. She had a blanket draped over her legs. Her Bible was open on her lap. But that's not the half of it. Their dining space adjoins the living room, creating one large room. And I have to report that it looked like a bomb had gone off in their living area! The floor was trashed. The table was covered and smeared with food and spilled milk. I maybe even spotted some spaghetti noodles hanging from the light fixture overhead and drooping off the backs of the chairs! The whole scene resembled a war zone!

Jim and I looked at the damage...and we looked at Courtney. And then she said, "You won't believe all that happened here after you left. I don't know what got into the kids, but they were awful. Everything got spilled or thrown. I finally got them down for their naps, and I was just sitting here trying to calm down and asking God to remind me of how much I love and wanted these children."

I personally think that my daughter found a fine solution that particular day to her real-life situation as a mother. She had the grace to know that her spiritual needs at that moment came first. Time spent finding comfort and confirmation from God's Word through her Bible and prayer was a priority...and a necessity! And she had the sense (again, thanks to God's grace) to just stop, leave things as they were, and look to the Lord for His patience and a quiet spirit. Plus she sought to maintain (or regain, whichever the case) her perspective on the blessings of having children to love and the privilege of parenting them. I have to say I was very Christian-proud of her that day. It appeared that she had "got it" in her understanding of God's plan and role for her as a Christian mother.

A Look at God's Calling to Love

A reminder—Dear reader, as we continue on in our quest for a better understanding of God's high calling to His women as spelled out in Titus 2:3-5, God points us next to the role of a mother: Christian women who are mothers are "to love their children." As one commentator notes about this high calling from God to *love*, "Love is the highest blessing in an earthly home, and of this the wife and mother is the natural center."[1]

However, while being devoted to husband and children should be a natural emotion, "many times depraved human nature succeeds in perverting such normal love."[2] Therefore, God *calls* all mothers "to love their children." And, since the older women have loved and raised their own children, He *calls* them to "assist the younger women in the discipline of family love."[3] The experienced mothers are *called* by God to teach and train new Christian mothers to give the teaching and training of their children a prominent place in their hearts and lives (and schedules!). And these older, wiser women are to literally *re-call* the young moms to their senses in the areas of the tasks, responsibilities, and privileges of motherhood. They are to instruct the young women with children to love their children in every way—"practical, physical, social, moral, and spiritual—with a love that has no conditions and no limits."[4]

Once again let's remember the setting of such instructions. The apostle Paul is writing to Titus. Titus was pastoring the churches on the island of Crete. The older, wiser Paul wrote this little letter to Titus to instruct him on how to have a healthy church. After dealing with the qualifications of leaders (Titus 1:5-9) and addressing the issue of false teachers (verses 10-16), Paul next turned his instruction to the positive ministry and teaching that should occur within the church. First, He addressed Titus as a pastor-teacher (Titus 2:1). Next, Paul laid out the conduct that should exemplify the older men and women in the church (verses 2 and 3). And now, as we step into verse 4, Paul has just charged the older women to be "teachers of good things" to the younger women. Furthermore, he has begun identifying what those "good things" are. So far in our study we've considered the first item on Paul's list—Christian wives are *to love their husbands*. And now we turn to the second item on the list of godly essentials for women—Christian mothers are *to love their children*.

A definition—What does it mean to *love* our children? Realize once again, as we focus on this significant high calling from God to us, that the words "to love their children" are used only here in the New Testament, in Titus 2:4. It is the same kind of love God calls us to regarding our husband—we are to love our children with *phileo* love, with a friendship love. Literally God's calling means mothers are to be *children-lovers*.[5] Such love is to flow out of the heart of a woman who's been saved by the love of Christ, who then extends Christ's love to her family first. The Christian woman's dear husband and children are to take first place in her heart.

And mothers are to turn to the older women for instruction and training in the outworkings of Christ's inward love. They are to learn from these wise women how to express sacrificial and selfless love toward their children. They are to seek for and submit to the more mature women in the body of Christ who have gone before them in the role of being a loving mother.

A decision—Does this information encourage you, dear friend? I hope so. I know it certainly encouraged me when I became a Christian at age 28 with a two-and-a-half-year-old and a one-and-a-half-year-old! I was clueless about not only how to be a Christian, but also how to be a Christian mother! But I made a decision—based on what I was learning from the passages in the Bible that speak directly to you and me as women (passages like the one from Titus 2 we're examining in this book)—that I would attend the classes at my church being taught by older women, that I would read the many good books written by Christians on raising godly children (and there are hundreds!), and that I would search out and meet with mothers who were ahead of me in the mothering race.

Our next chapter will contain godly advice about Christian parenting from a variety of sources. But before you finish reading this chapter, I would like to call you to make a decision—actually two decisions:

Decision #1—A decision to be taught Christian mothering by an older Christian woman, and

Decision #2—A decision to teach Christian mothering to younger Christian women.

As we move through God's high calling to the older women to *teach* and His high calling to the younger women to *learn*, how can you and I fail to make these decisions? I mean, don't we want to answer God's high calling to love our children and to teach others to do the same thing? Don't we want to factor in this essential for godly living, the essential of being a loving mother and a teacher to others?

Oh please! Don't continue on without making your own decision about these essential matters!

A Look at God's Teaching

You and I can thank God that His Word speaks clearly to us as parents about godly parenting. I want us to now look at four scriptures on this vital subject.

1. *Deuteronomy 6:6-7*—Moses wrote these instructions in the law of the Old Testament: "And these words which I command you today shall be in your heart; you shall teach them diligently to your children, and shall talk of them when you sit in your house, when you walk by the way, when you lie down, and when you rise up."

    Here God's law requires parents, first of all, to *take* His law into their own hearts, and second, to *talk* of His law day and night, day-in and day-out, both inside and outside the home to their sons and daughters. In others words, godly parents are to teach and talk of the things of the Lord to their children throughout each and every day and act of life...until those children in turn have children of their own and begin the cycle of godly instruction all over again to a new generation.

While a good church and a Christian school may assist us as Christian parents in the teaching and training of our children, God places the sole responsibility on us, the parents. We, as the *parents*, are to *diligently* teach and train our own children.

2. *Proverbs 1:8*—"My son, hear the instruction of your father, and do not forsake the law of your mother"—*and 6:20*—"My son, keep your father's command, and do not forsake the law of your mother."

What is a godly mother? A godly mother is one who loves the Lord her God with all *her* heart, soul, mind, and strength and then passionately, consistently, and unrelentingly teaches her *offspring* to do the same. No one has more potential for godly influence on a child than that child's God-fearing mother. So, dear mother, we are to take up the cause, answer God's call, muster up our courage, and set out to be the best, most faithful teacher of God's Word and God's ways to our precious children. And we must pray—each and every day and all along the way—for God to empower us to do so and to empower His Word in the soft soil of our little ones' hearts.

God's roll call of godly mothers is long and impressive. We'll look later to the mothers of Jesus, Moses, Samuel, and Timothy. Plus, think of—and thank God for—the mothers of such Christian leaders as Augustine (Monica) and the brothers John and Charles Wesley (Susanna). Your calling, my reading sister, young or old, is to join their ranks and *teach* those little ones nearest to you—the ones right in your own family and home!

3.   *1 Timothy 2:15*—"She will be saved in child-
     bearing if they continue in faith, love, and holi-
     ness, with self-control." This verse is not about
     the eternal salvation of the soul from sin, which
     is only through Jesus Christ. Rather it is about the
     salvation of woman's dignity and honor, which
     were lost when she was tempted and deceived by
     the serpent in Genesis 3 (see 1 Timothy 2:14).
     Actually, "saved" is better translated "preserved."
     As my pastor puts it, "Paul is teaching that even
     though a woman bears the stigma of being the
     initial instrument that led the race into sin, it is
     women through childbearing who may be pre-
     served or freed from that stigma by raising a gen-
     eration of godly children.... While a woman may
     have led the human race into sin, women have
     the privilege of leading many out of sin to godli-
     ness."[6]

     If you are a mother, you have a most won-
derful task before you in positively influencing
the generations to come for Jesus Christ! Hear
how a few familiar stanzas of poetry express this
influence:

They say that man is mighty,
He governs land and sea,
He wields a mighty scepter
O'er lesser powers than he.

But a mighty power and stronger
Man from His throne has hurled:
For the hand that rocks the cradle
Is the hand that rules the world.
                              —William Wallace[7]

4.   *Titus 2:3-4*—"...that [the older women] admonish
the young women...to love their children." Hopefully by now you're getting a handle on the
meaning—and the calling—of what this love for
your children entails. There are no conditions.
And there are no if's, and's, or but's. And there
are no excuses. As Christian mothers we are to
love our children...regardless...no matter what...
period. It's our high calling! And where does such
love come from? It is to spring forth from a holy,
sanctified heart and extend itself freely to our
children—not based upon their looks, their per-
sonalities, their brilliance, nor their response to
our attempts to love. And, dear faithful mother, it
will take *all* of God's rich abundant grace and *all*
that we can give to accomplish such a high
calling. Loving our children may well be the
hardest work-in-the-Lord we ever do! And based
on 1 Timothy 2:15, it is our greatest work-in-the-
Lord!

A Sampling of Loving Mothers

In my search for models who fulfilled God's "words" to
you and me about godly mothering, I turned to the study of
the women of the Bible. Here's just a sampling of what I
found there among God's gallery of loving mothers.

*Sarah, Rebekah, Rachel, Hannah, Samson's mother, and
Elizabeth* (to name a few)—all desperately wanted to have
children. In fact, Rachel said to her husband Jacob, "Give me
children, or else I die!" (Genesis 30:1). These women knew
that children are a good thing, a blessing from God. God
Himself moved the psalmist to declare, "Lo, children are a

heritage from the Lord; the fruit of the womb is His reward....
Happy is the man who has his quiver full of them" (Psalm
127:3,5).

Jochebed—bore and mothered the little infant Moses
(Exodus 2). A mother who deeply cherished her baby boy,
Jochebed hid him to save his little life from the Pharaoh's
edict that all Hebrew babies should be murdered. After three
months, she placed him in an ark of bulrushes and set him
at the edge of the river. Later, by the providence of God,
she was allowed to nurse and nurture Moses until about age
three when she turned him over to be raised by Pharaoh's
daughter in the ruler's palace. Because she was a mother
who lived out God's high calling to love her children,
Jochebed was, by the grace of God, able to impart to her
little toddler enough truth about the living God that later he
renounced the ways of Pharaoh's household and became
perhaps the greatest leader of God's people. Oh, the power
and penetration of a mother's instruction to the little ones
upon her knee!

Hannah—was an outstanding mother who also only
had her little boy Samuel to mother for about three years
(1 Samuel 1). At that tender age, Hannah presented Samuel
to the priest Eli at the house of the Lord in Shiloh where he
was raised to serve the Lord (1 Samuel 2), later becoming
one of God's dynamic prophets and priests. Evidently the
loving instruction Hannah passed on to this little tike was
implanted deeply enough to enable Samuel to stand strong
in character even while surrounded by the ungodly influence of Eli and his two corrupt sons. Again, never underestimate the power and penetration of a mother's instruction
to the little ones upon her knee!

Mary, the mother of Jesus—was the woman favored and chosen by God to miraculously bear His only begotten son (Luke 1:28). Jesus' home life and training in those times began with the keeping of Moses' law by Mary and Joseph in the rite of circumcision, His presentation and dedication to God, and the offering of the sacrifices prescribed by the law (Luke 2:21-24). The Bible gives evidence that the mother did much of the training of her children in their initial years (Proverbs 31:1 and 2 Timothy 3:15). Early training was delegated by the Mosaic law to Jewish parents—the home was the school and the parents were the teachers. Later children generally attended the synagogue school. There the Bible, the Law, and theology were taught. Family pilgrimages to worship (Luke 2:41-42) and the recitation of "The Shema," a prayer quoting passages from the Pentateuch, were also parts of the religious training that took place in the home.[8] Surely Mary, who identified herself as "the maidservant of the Lord" (Luke 1:38), carefully followed through on each and every requirement of the Jewish law!

Eunice—was the godly mother of Timothy. Married to an unbelieving Greek, this woman was able to pass on "the genuine faith" (Acts 16:1 and 2 Timothy 1:5) to her son Timothy. The apostle Paul remarked to Timothy that "from childhood you have known the Holy Scriptures, which are able to make you wise for salvation through faith which is in Christ Jesus" (2 Timothy 3:15). Eunice—with the Lord's help—had done the greatest and most loving thing any Christian mother can do for her child: She taught Timothy the Scriptures and introduced him to the saving knowledge of Jesus Christ.

Lois—shares the stage with her daughter Eunice in the raising of little Timothy. Paul included this maternal grandmother when he wrote to Timothy, "I call to remembrance the genuine faith that is in you, which dwelt first in your grandmother Lois and your mother Eunice" (2 Timothy 1:5). (I, for one, have heard many women share that their greatest loss in life was the death of a grandmother. I've sat through many baptisms and listened to women testify that their godly grandmother was the one who loved them, loved God, and showed them God's love, ever pointing them to the Savior. Oh, may we who are grandmothers never underestimate the godly influence and teaching we can pass on to our dear little grand-ones!)

As we leave these shining examples of mothers who faithfully and lovingly taught and trained their precious children, we should be touched in our own hearts as we contemplate the role and responsibility God has given to us as mothers... and the impact we can have upon our children as we love them for Christ's sake. An unknown writer of old explained it most eloquently:

> The mother in her office holds the key of the soul; and she it is who stamps the coin of character and makes the being who would be a savage, but for her gentle cares, a Christian man! Then crown her queen of the world.[9]

Looking Upward

Oh, dear mother! Far from being an inferior or a secondary calling, our calling to be loving and godly mothers is indeed most high! No one else is called to love our children but us. And no one else can love our children like us. God calls you and me to love our God-given children. *How* they came to be ours doesn't matter. The fact that they *are* ours means that they are to be loved. So, dear one, I see God's high calling as being fivefold: If you have children, you are to:

1. *Love* them and make loving them your highest pursuit.

2. *Look* to the Word of God for His guidelines for being a loving Christian mother.

3. *Look* at the modeling of older Christian women as they express Christlike love to their children.

4. *Look* to the older Christian women to teach you the how-to's of such love.

5. *Learn* from such women.

Then by God's grace you just might...

> *Leave* your mark on the world by leaving behind a child who grows up to love and serve the Lord...who then also raises godly children to continue your godly legacy for generations to come.

Essential 6

"...admonish the young women to love their...children..."
—TITUS 2:4

"The most important responsibility of love for believing parents is to lead their children to a saving knowledge of Jesus Christ."
—JOHN MACARTHUR

"The world is tugging at our children's hearts, pulling them down and away from God. Loving our children means we are willing to get down in the trenches and fight to turn our children's hearts toward God—toward His Word and His ways."

Chapter Twelve

Loving Your Family—An Essential for Godly Living

ears ago, when my own two precious God-given daughters were little girls, I read (and saved) this anonymous poem found in a biography of the life of Dr. Henrietta Mears. Dr. Mears served as the Director of Christian Education at the famed Hollywood Presbyterian Church in California. Never marrying, this devoted-to-Christ and devoted-to-children lady was enabled by God as the director of the Sunday schools to "mold" the souls and hearts of the many young people (people such as Bill Bright, founder of Campus Crusade for Christ ministries) who attended her Sunday school class. Perhaps you'll want to save this poignant poem too.

A Piece of Plastic Clay

I took a piece of plastic clay
And idly fashioned it one day,
And as my fingers pressed it still,
It moved and yielded to my will.

I came again when days were passed;
The bit of clay was hard at last,
The form I gave it still it bore,
But I could change that form no more.

I took a piece of living clay
And touched it gently day by day,
And molded with my power and art
A young child's soft and yielding heart.

I came again when years were gone;
It was a mind I looked upon;
That early impress still he wore,
And I could change that form no more.

Henrietta Mears was a woman who served God her whole life long shaping the lives of the children of others for Christ. Now the question is, if *you* are a mother, are *you* doing the same for *your* dear sons and daughters?

Nothing—and no one—is more near and dear to my heart than my family. And if you're a mother, I'm sure you feel the same way. But you and I must be careful of T-I-M-E! Time is subtle. It appears to be passing slowly—too slowly for our impatient ways! As young moms we stand at the front end of family life, a life overflowing with babies, bottles, diapers, and a draining lack of sleep. This phase of parenting seems to drag on...only to dully transition into a new one filled with spilled food and overturned milk cups, potty training, discipline, and a house that seems to never be clutter-free. If we're not careful, we can wish and while these days away—these very few precious, God-given days available for forming the soft, yielding hearts of our children. (Remember Jochebed and Hannah, devoted mothers who only had about three years with their little guys!)

We can so easily get caught up in trying to hurry our life (and our children's lives!) along, to get past these seemingly unimportant and sometimes bothersome days. We can yearn for the gruesome career of at-home parenting to end so that we can "get on with real life." And the first thing you know, we've entrusted our little ones to a babysitter or enrolled them in a play school several days a week or even every morning.

In reality, though, both you and I know that time is speeding by. And more quickly than we think! Our days can easily become filled with simply allowing time to pass by while we fail to take seriously the brief time we actually have to teach and train our children. Before we know it, their soft and yielding hearts harden into a mind and a character that is set for life.

So, what can you do while time is passing? What can you do to make the minutes, months, and years count? As a mother whose little girls have grown up to become mothers themselves, let me share a mixture of what I did, what others did, and what my daughters are doing now to live out God's high calling to love our children. Whether yours are little or not-so-little ones, these God-ordained, time-honored biblical means make a difference—a tremendous difference!

Ten Ways to Love Your Children

1. *Teach them.* I meet a lot of moms (and dads!) who give great attention, spend vast sums of money, and schedule large amounts of time to ensure that their children are adequately taught how to play baseball, basketball, or soccer; how to play the piano, to sing, dance, or tumble— even how to properly "take tea." They make sure

their children master certain skills and develop hobbies. They make sure their kids—from infancy to the altar—are wearing the "right" clothes, the "with-it" brands and styles. Even the tiny ones *must* know all about "Blues Clues" and be on a first-name basis with each character on "Sesame Street." Oh, no, they wouldn't want *their* child to be perceived as a freak or a geek. No, they must be "with it," be "cool."

On and on the list of worldly "must knows" goes. But the weightier things—the fundamentals of the Christian life—things like going to church, memorizing Bible verses and hymns, learning how to have daily devotions, how to pray, how to give at church, how to serve others, how to help people, how to extend mercy and compassion, are treated as secondary or are completely absent.

Dear Christian mother, we *must* wake up to the awesome responsibility we have to teach our children! We *must* make our Christian "must know" list. And once the list is made we *must* set about to teach our children how to live like Christians. They *must* know about Jesus—who He is and the fact of His sacrificial death on their behalf. Our earnest plea to God *must* be for the salvation of our children's souls—and our instruction *must* earnestly point them toward the One who is able to accomplish that salvation.

And, speaking of "waking up" to the awesome responsibility we have to teach our children, hear these sobering words from my husband's friends, Dennis and Dawn Wilson.

> The Puritans' devout love of God, their obedience and allegiance to the Scriptures, and their eternal perspective of

their children gave them a sense of parental responsibility and stewardship that greatly surpasses that of today's cultural Christianity. Their words of challenge written centuries ago should cut us to the heart:

"It is in your hands to do them the greatest kindness or cruelty in all the world: help them to know God and to be saved, and you do more for them than if you helped them to be lords or princes: if you neglect their souls, and breed them in ignorance, worldliness, ungodliness, and sin, you betray them to the devil, the enemy of souls, even as truly as if you sold them to him; you sell them to be slaves to Satan; you betray them to him that will deceive them and abuse them in this life, and torment them in the next."[1]

Now, do these words give you a little different—and more eternal—perspective on your high calling to be a teacher of the truth?!

Dear privileged-and-called-by-God mother, our role of "teacher" is not optional. No, as we learned in the previous chapter, it is commanded by God. It's another one of His high callings to women who have little ones (and big ones, too... and grand-ones also!). So, do *you*, precious mom, love God enough to pay the price to earnestly seek to fulfill His command to you to teach your children about Him? And do you love your *children* enough to sacrifice...

> your self (it will cost *you* personally to put
> this discipline in place),
> your time (lesser pursuits will have to
> make way for the greater),
> your energy (training is rewarding work...
> but never easy work), and
> your money (Bibles and books and music
> and materials will have to be obtained
> to help aim your teaching of God's
> truth straight into your youngsters'
> hearts)?

It will cost all of this—and more—plus adequate
preparation and consistent scheduling to ensure
that your children know all about the greatest
thing in the world—God's love for them and His
instructions on how they should live their lives.

2. *Train them.* Certainly every mother should train
her children to work and fulfill their responsibilities and do things "heartily" and with a good attitude. But even more important than such vital
instruction for life is training our offspring to
obey—to obey what the Bible teaches, to obey
their father, and to obey you, their mother. (And I
have to comment here that I cannot count the
times I've heard my two daughters tell their little
ones, "You must obey Poppy and Mimi." They are
being trained to do what Jim and I, their grand-
parents, ask of them.)

Children also need to learn—and must be
trained—to respect their teachers, to respect
authority, to cooperate with others, as well as fulfill their responsibilities. As author and pastor
Chuck Swindoll writes, we must "hold their feet to
the fire." We must hold our children accountable to

faithfulness in their obligations at home, at school, at work, and at church.

Dear mom, your teaching is crucial and your training is critical, for "the instruction received at the mother's knee, and the paternal lessons, together with the pious and sweet souvenirs of the fireside, are never effaced entirely from the soul."[2]

3. *Talk to God about them.* I briefly mentioned Monica earlier, but here I want to be specific about this pious woman's inspiring life of prayer for her family. Monica was a woman—a wife and a mother of three children—who lived her 56 years between 331 and 387 A.D. One of her children was Augustine, a wayward son who became a man of fiery temper and immoral habits. At school he joined the most unruly crowd and openly spurned the Christian teachings of his mother, choosing to move deeply into sin.

Nevertheless, Augustine's saintly mother patiently persevered in prayer for her debauched son. Yet Augustine evaded her and mocked her Christian teachings and prayers. When he decided to leave Carthage and go to Rome, Monica wished to accompany him, going with him as far as the seaport. But her conniving son tricked his sincere mother into spending the night in a church. By morning he was on his way to Rome, and Monica was left behind. Sorrowfully but prayerfully she went home. Her persistent prayers were answered when, in Milan, Italy, the persuasive preaching of the great Bishop Ambrose (mixed with the incense of a mother's faithful supplications to God on behalf of her son) finally won Augustine to Christ at the age of 33.

It's reported that upon hearing of Augustine's rebirth, the dear mother said, "Now I can die." Sadly, on the trip to join her son after his conversion and baptism, she did just that.

In the end, Monica's faith, prayers, and Christian life helped influence her whole family to become Christians. Augustine became one of the greatest and most influential of the early Church Fathers. Before she died, this saintly, loving mother saw her three children and her husband all become Christians.

Precious reader and precious mother, to love our children is to pray for them. Yes, we *teach* and we *train*, but we also *talk to God* about them. Even if our sons or daughters cease to listen to us, God never does! Are you a praying mother? Would you pray 33 years if your child were wayward, cruel, demeaning, and corrupt? Beloved, we are called by God to love our children...no matter what. And love prays!

4. *Talk to them about God.* Of course we should talk to God about our children, but we should also talk to our children about God. That's the instruction of Deuteronomy 6:6-7—you are to talk to your sons and daughters about God "when you sit in your house, when you walk by the way, when you lie down, and when you rise up." We should *take* every opportunity to talk about God—and we should *make* opportunities to talk about God.

5. *Take time to read on mothering.* During the days of my own discipleship ministry to younger women, not only did I have each married woman read five minutes a day on marriage, but each

woman who had children was also required to read five minutes a day on child raising. Why? To keep them sharp as moms. To keep them on their toes in their training of their young ones. To keep them thinking about their high calling as mothers. To keep them in touch with experts in the area of child raising. To keep them actively reaching to do a better job, eagerly and energetically pressing forward in their mothering duties, and keenly committed to faithfully following after their high calling of being a godly mother.

I want to recommend the same exercise for you, my friend. Read...and read...and read some more! And file away what you're reading. In time, you'll want to refer back to it yourself if the Lord folds more children into your family and when, Lord willing, you turn up next in line to teach the younger moms what you've learned! What a wonderful day that will be!

6. *Take time to read to them.* I know many parents who routinely read classical children's literature to their little ones. As a former English literature teacher, I had a list of the top 100 children's books that are considered foundational to a child's education. But our first priority—as a *godly* mother, as a *Christian* parent, as a believer who holds in our hands God's high calling to love, to teach, to train (etc.) His children—*must* be reading God's Word, God's stories, and good books about Jesus to such tender, pliable, moldable minds! They *must* know about the Bible and its heroes. The God-inspired words of the Bible *must* take root in our precious youngsters' hearts! Oh, may their dreams and aspirations be filled with the examples of men and women who have

faithfully served God...instead of puppets and cartoon figures, instead of caped and masked superheroes, instead of teen idols and rock stars!

7. *Teach them to pray*. Here are some startling words I read (and saved—are you getting the picture?) when I was in the throes of motherhood.

> The heathen mother takes her babe to the idol temple, and teaches it to clasp its little hands before its forehead, in the attitude of prayer, long before it can utter a word. As soon as it can walk, it is taught to gather a few flowers or fruits, or put a little rice upon a banana-leaf, and lay them upon the altar before the idol god. As soon as it can utter the names of its parents, so soon it is taught to offer up its petitions before the images. Who ever saw a heathen child that could speak, and not pray?
>
> Christian mothers, why is it that so many children grow up in this enlightened land without learning to pray?[3]

If this scene is true (and we know it is!) then why-oh-why, dear Christian mother, do we wait—or fail—to teach our toddlers to pray?! I know that my little grandson Jacob learned to scrunch his eyes shut and bury his head into his clasped hands during "grace" well before he was one. And my little Taylor Jane's mom had to cover Taylor's mouth at church because she loved to yell out "Amen!" every time anyone prayed during the worship service! She was a mere one-year-old, but she was already well familiar with "praying" at home.

8. *Take care of them.* We'll spend more time considering the works of love done at and in the home in several chapters yet to come, but for now take to heart that "loving" your children means taking care of them. Food, clothes, rest, a safe home, order, a schedule, a place of peace are your children's rights. And you, as the mother, are the provider of such care. And it will take all that you are and can give—empowered by God's energy and grace—to do so! As my daughter Katherine said to me one day when I remarked that she looked a little tired, "Oh, Mom, I've been tired since the day Taylor was born!" That about says it all when it comes to the sacrificial price God calls His mothers to make for their brood.

9. *Tell them about Jesus.* On the list of *must* and *have-to's* for you and me as mothers who are seeking to answer God's high calling to love our children is telling them about Jesus. Why? So they know about the love of Jesus for them (John 3:16) and so that they can love Him, too. This chapter is about God's high calling to *love* our children, and, as my pastor writes, "The most important responsibility of *love* for believing parents is to lead their *children* to a saving knowledge of Jesus Christ."[4] I pray that your little ones hear enough about Jesus to begin begging you to "tell me the stories of Jesus." You may recognize this as the title of a an old-time hymn. Its author, William H. Parker, returned home from church one Sunday after teaching his Sunday school class. As he reflected upon his class's constant cry of "Teacher, tell us another story!" he wrote his famous hymn on that Lord's day afternoon in 1885. Notice how it covers the broad spectrum of the life, the teachings, and the death of the Savior.

Tell Me the Stories of Jesus

Tell me the stories of Jesus I love to hear;
Things I would ask Him to tell me,
        if He were here:
Scenes by the wayside, tales of the sea,
Stories of Jesus, tell them to me.

First let me hear how the children
        stood 'round His knee;
And I shall fancy His blessing resting on me:
Words full of kindness, deeds full of grace,
All in the lovelight of Jesus' face.

Into the city I'd follow the children's band,
Waving a branch of the palm tree high
        in my hand;
One of His heralds, yes, I would sing
Loudest hosannas! Jesus is King.

Show me that scene in the garden, of bitter pain.
Show me the cross where my Savior for me
        was slain.
Sad ones or bright ones, so that they be
Stories of Jesus, tell them to me.

Children love to hear stories! Why not as a loving mother—one who loves Jesus yourself—make sure that you take advantage of your child's keen interest in stories and fill his or her mind with truths about Jesus? Why not allow the stories of Jesus to lay a firm foundation upon which each child may build his life? Why not simply tell your precious one the stories of Jesus?

10. *Try your best—with the Lord's help—to model god-liness.* If you're a woman seeking to follow after

God and answer His high callings, I'm sure you're already making strides in this sphere of modeling a spiritual life before your children. Truly, the most valuable gift you can give your family is a good example!

Looking Upward

Beloved, there are tens of tens of ways to love your children! I am trusting (and praying!) that after reading through these two chapters you better understand what a privilege and high calling it is to have and to love children.

But the primary way for you and me to love our children is to go to war, to do spiritual battle on their behalf. There can be no greater testimony of a mother's love, care, and concern than her campaign for the spiritual welfare of her child. Such was the apostle Paul's observation of his protégé Timothy's godly mother and grandmother, that from childhood Timothy had known the Holy Scriptures, which were able to make him wise for salvation through faith which is in Christ Jesus (2 Timothy 3:15).

As we look upward here before we move on in our exploration of God's high callings, consider again the importance of this singular calling to parenting, as explained by author Tedd Tripp in his best-selling book, *Shepherding a Child's Heart*—parents are engaged "in hand-to-hand combat on the world's smallest battlefield, the child's heart."[5] The world is tugging at our children's hearts, pulling them down and away from God. Loving our children means we are willing to get down in the trenches and fight to turn our children's hearts toward God—toward His Word and His ways.

May you, dear precious mother, ever look upward—for God's almighty strength and empowering grace—and may you ever fight the good fight of faith (1 Timothy 6:12)! Your child's heart is at stake!

Essential 7

"...admonish the young women...
to be discreet..."
—TITUS 2:4-5

"The woman who is wise is a woman who is
sober-*minded*, well-*minded*, sound-*minded*.
Passions and thoughts are under control, therefore she is self-controlled and of sound mind,
acting with wisdom."

"Wisdom keeps her eye on her heart, on her
homefront, and on heaven. Wisdom gives
diligent attention to being *who God wants her to
be in her heart*, to doing *what God wants her to
do on her homefront*, and to doing *the things
that count for eternity in heaven*. This is what
wisdom is all about."

"Peace and order and simplicity can be ours
if we will seek to answer God's high calling to
walk in wisdom, if we practice our priorities and
pursue balance in life's prerequisites."

Chapter Thirteen

A Woman's High Calling to Wisdom

ould you like to hear a joke? A Bible joke? Or should I say, a joke out of the Bible?

In case you didn't know there was such a thing as a joke in the Bible, here it is: "As a ring of gold in a swine's snout, so is a lovely woman who lacks discretion" (Proverbs 11:22). Believe it or not, this is a joke. The subject of this proverb is a beautiful woman who lacks discretion and common sense. And the absurdity of the joke is that a lovely woman who acts foolishly is as unattractive and as inappropriate as a filthy, unclean pig with an expensive jeweled nose-ring in its snout!

We'll get back to the writer of this proverb and his use of jest and sarcasm to make a point later. For now, though, let the bejeweled pig image simmer for a while as we look into our next essential for godly living—God's high calling to *wisdom*. Paul writes to Titus that the older women are to "admonish the young women...to be discreet" (Titus 2:3-5).

A Calling to All Christians

As we approach this new calling, it helps us to know about the word itself, *sophron*. This Greek word *sophron* is translated as *discreet, temperate, self-controlled, sober, sober-minded, sensible, reasonable, wise,* and *orderly.* For our purposes, I am choosing to use the word *wise.* It's a familiar word and a term that seems to wrap its arms around all the other synonymous meanings.

And *who* is called to be wise and self-controlled and discreet? Answer—*all* Christians are called to such character! For instance, note these "callings" out of the book of Titus:

—Elders or overseers are called to be wise and self-controlled (Titus 1:8).

—Older men are called to be wise and sober (Titus 2:2).

—Older women are called to teach the younger women to be wise and discreet, which implies that the older women possess wisdom themselves (Titus 2:3).

—Young women are called to be wise and discreet (Titus 2:5).

—All believers are called to live in a wise manner or soberly (Titus 2:12).

As we can clearly see, God's calling to live wisely—soberly, discreetly, and in a controlled manner—is truly an important calling to *all* Christians! In fact, it's essential!

A Calling to Wisdom As a Lifestyle

And what does God's calling for wise behavior mean? What a word! And what a life it would be if we submitted ourselves to be taught and trained and dedicated to live wisely! To grasp what God has in mind for you and me as His women, I want us to look at...

First, the word—The word we're considering is the Greek word *sophron*, a combination of *sozo* = safe and sound and well, and *phren* = heart, mind, and thought. The heart is the seat of the passions, the place where the activities of the soul are located, the place where we feel. And the mind is where we think. Therefore, the woman who is wise is a woman who is *sober*-minded, *well*-minded, *sound*-minded. Passions and thoughts are under control—therefore, she is self-controlled and of sound mind, acting with wisdom.

Next, some meanings—Take a minute to read through some of the many shades of meaning for disciplined wisdom. Wisdom and discretion...

   ...has the idea of self-control.[1]
   ...has to do with personal character, with being
      sober-minded. The young women are to be
      balanced in act and judgment, discreet in all
      their relations.[2]
   ...means to be prudent.[3]
   ...means to be discreet. Outlook determines out-
      come; and if a person is not thinking rightly, he
      will not act properly. A woman needs a cor-
      rect and disciplined outlook. Self-controlled is
      the idea contained in this word.[4]
   ...is the Christian virtue of self-control.[5]

...means to be sensible, to possess common sense
    and good judgment.[6]
...means sober-minded or better, discreet. Perhaps
    the French *sage* is nearer still.[7]
...means wise and careful in conduct.[8]
...points to sobriety or wisdom; that calm quietude
    of heart and mind which is not intoxicated by
    vanity, or carried away with the sensationalism
    of pleasure.[9]

Finally, some opposites—Looking at the opposites of a particular quality teaches us much. In the case of wisdom and
discretion, some opposites are *foolishness, rashness, overly
enthusiastic, impulsive, emotional,* and *improper.*

I'm sure you can see right away that these childish qualities have *no* place in the life of God's women, of Christian
women, of women who are seeking to live in a godly
manner, a manner that brings honor to God's name (Titus
2:5)! I know I've been seriously attempting to put away such
childish behaviors (1 Corinthians 13:11) from my lifestyle for
a *long* time. Oh, we all have our moments, our bloops and
our blunders! But I thank God that there are fewer and fewer
of them as time has graciously passed and taught me a few
lessons along the way.

Wisdom is an essential for godly living. Wouldn't you
agree? May you and I not be guilty of improper conduct, of
speaking foolishness and foolishly, of rashly running ahead
of the Lord's (and/or our husband's!) plans, of acting before
we ask (ask the Lord...and our husband...or an older
woman or wise counselor), of letting it all "hang out" and
giving in to the spewing of ungodly speech, to words that
cut like "the piercings of a sword" (Proverbs 12:18), to
impulse and emotion or to peer pressure(!). May it never be
said of us, "Hey, did you hear the one about the pig with the
jewel in its nose?! Did you hear the one about the lovely
lady who was a fool?!"

And now for some how-to's and practical tips and suggestions for gaining ground in this vital area of godliness and maturity. Let's begin putting God's high calling to us to be women of wisdom to work in our daily life right now.

Marks of a Woman of Wisdom

I'm sure there are many telltale marks of a woman of wisdom, but several stand out to me immediately.

#1. She knows her priorities...and practices them. If you and I are to walk through life as women of wisdom, we must know what God sets down in His Word as His priorities for us. Indeed, that's what Titus 2:3-5 is all about! It's our God-given assignment for all of life. It's about the way God wants us to live our life, the relationships God wants us to establish and improve, and the character qualities God wants us to pursue.

And what are our priorities? Titus 2:3-5 says we are to set our sights on and our energies to work in these specific areas:

> Verse 3—godly behavior and reverence
> godly speech (no gossip!)
> personal discipline (moderation in
> all things) and
> encouraging and instructing other
> women
>
> Verse 4—family love toward husband and
> children
> Verse 5—wisdom and sensibility
> homemaking
> purity
> goodness and
> obedience to husbands

Summed up, these essentials for godly living set three life-time and lifelong goals for you and me.

Goal #1:   We are to cultivate godly conduct and behavior.

Goal #2:   We are to cultivate family relationships that honor the Lord.

Goal #3:   We are to cultivate godly character qualities.

While the items on this list of priorities may appear to be "all over the place," they encompass what God has in mind for us as His women. They are *the* essentials for His women. They reveal *His* will for our life. They also encompass the varying ages and stages we will pass through in our lifetime—from young woman to older woman.

As I think about such high goals and God's high calling for us, my mind races to the woman in Proverbs 31:10-31 who has always served for me as a model of godliness in both heart and home. Her list of godly character qualities is *long!* And her relationships at home were *strong!* And her conduct was such that a chorus of praise was lifted by her blessed family and by all in the gates of her community (Proverbs 31:28-31). Of her it has been written, "The woman celebrated [in Proverbs 31] is the one who realizes in all fullness and richness the capacities and glories of her womanhood."[10] Dear one, such a statement is realized by you and me, too, when we seek with all our heart, soul, mind, and strength to answer God's few-but-high callings to us.

So, how can we set our sights on these things from above, on these few essentials from the heart and mind of God? I would say this: Wisdom keeps her eye on her heart, on her homefront, and on heaven. Wisdom gives diligent attention to *being* who God wants her to be in her heart, to *doing* what God wants her to do on her homefront, and to *doing* the things that count for eternity in heaven. This is what wisdom is all about. Ask God to help you trim out of your life what is meaningless, trivial, and secondary. True, many of the things we do and the pursuits we choose are *fun*. But do they matter? Do they make a meaningful contribution to *any*one? To your family? And do they really matter to God and in heaven? From God's perspective? Do they really possess *eternal* value?

I've made it a quest of mine to focus on the few things that the Bible plainly says really matter to God and to my family and to the body of Christ. It just seems that there is so little time...and increasingly less energy...to give to *any* pursuits! Therefore, I carefully and prayerfully seek to choose the best-of-the-best options for my minutes and my strength. That, beloved reader, is what wisdom is—choosing to live life according to the priorities God sets down for His women. That's the definition of discretion, of sensibility, of wisdom. As another has written,

> Wisdom is the ability to use the best means at the best time to accomplish the best ends. It is not merely a matter of information or knowledge, but of skillful and practical application of the truth to the ordinary facets of life.[11]

By God's grace, making His best choices is how you and I can be women who walk in wisdom.

#2. She is balanced in every area of life—I like the definition we considered above written by the gentleman who wrote that wisdom means to be *balanced*. If I had to list my top-ten pursuits (maybe even my top-five!), one of them would be balance. Do you ever wonder how to fit everything into an already crowded life? Well, I do. And in that quest I seek balance, beautiful balance! I talk to so many women who yearn to give the fundamentals of life equal

force, to fit them all in, to find an even keel in handling all of the areas of life.

And what are these keynote areas of life? Believe me, I've given this question a lot of prayerful thought and research over the past few decades. I would say that the few fundamentals of life include these:

Spiritual life— loving God first and foremost, with all our heart, soul, strength, and mind (Luke 10:27)

Family life— loving and serving those at home first (Titus 2:4-5)

Home life— taking good care of the place where our loved ones live (Titus 2:5)

Church life— discovering, developing, and using our spiritual gifts (1 Corinthians 12:7)

Physical life— making sure the "vessel"—the body—is fit and able to serve the Lord and others (1 Corinthians 9:27)

Social life—fitting in time for friends and neighbors (Proverbs 18:24; Luke 10:27)

Financial life—being a wise steward of what God has given us (Matthew 25:21)

Mental life— using our mind to grow and to glorify God (Romans 15:4 and Psalm 19:14)

Again, the Proverbs 31 woman comes to mind. This wonderful woman seemed to fit it all in! One reading through Proverbs 31:10-31 reveals this fact. For indeed, she was a woman who feared the Lord, loved and cared for her husband and children, took great care of her home, maintained a ministry to her community, used her mind to manage her life and her homefront, and helped handle the family finances. Why, she even had strong arms!

As I've sought balance in my life and fought to manage the necessities and requirements of life, one exercise has catapulted me (for the first time) into a more successful treatment of these eight areas of my life. It's a simple weekly exercise using a simple weekly calendar. I've had lifetime and yearly goals in each of these eight areas, but the question and challenge has always been, "How can I live them out each week? Each day?" So now, every Sunday afternoon I write these eight headings in my weekly calendar. Next, I set a weekly goal in each area. Then I schedule each day of the week to reflect the eight goals. I determine what time and/or what day I'll do each one of them.

Here's a little sampling of this week's attempts at balance.

Spiritual—Have devotions each morning and write in my personal journal. Right now I am thoroughly enjoying going through *The One Year Book of Psalms.*[12]

Family—My daughters now have families of their own, but this past week I sent a goodie box off to New York City (Katherine and family) and made plans to visit Washington (Courtney and family). This is, of course, in addition to emails and phone calls. Also, we're planning a family reunion for Thanksgiving (I'm already at work on that—it won't be easy, but then, nurturing family ties never is!). Plus several times a week I share emails with my three brothers as the four of us look after my 93-year-old mother, the only living parent Jim and I still have.

Home—Well, the termite man was just here to treat the wood frame around our garage. Now we need to paint the trim. So this week's "home" list included the removal of the creeping fig ivy growing around the entrance to our house...so that (next week's "home" list) we can begin lining up the painting! (Not real exciting—but very needful. And all of this is being done with a long eye on the future family reunion at Thanksgiving!)

Church—This week was our church's annual pastors' conference. And just last evening Jim and I were involved in our missions outreach to our international visitors, meeting and greeting all those who traveled from foreign countries to attend the conference.

Physical—All I can say in this area is that I *try* every week! I write down the same four words every Sunday—walk, exercise, vitamins, and diet (sometimes this one is more specific—like lose one pound). Each item then becomes a daily goal to be checked off. Plus this week's list includes some fasting for annual blood work. Oh yes—and a much-needed haircut!

Social—I'm not sure I like this word, because "social butterfly" always comes to mind. And believe me, that's not me! But *social* is a good word that encompasses both friends and acquaintances. Every week I write down the names of my five best friends, and then every week I try to call and communicate with each of them in some way. I regret that many a week flies by without the much-desired contact...but at least I'm trying! They're busy people, and so am I. So staying in touch is always a goal for all parties. Plus I try to stay current on the many thank-you notes I need to write.

Financial—Today's date is March 10...and you know what happens on April 15! It's tax time! So we're busy rounding up the figures from last year for tax preparation. (And, of course, praying!)

Mental—My next (Lord willing!) Bible study release is scheduled to be Judges and Ruth, so this week the research books were ordered, and next week the studying and writing begin!

As a word of testimony, let me say that I've tried all kinds of planners and devices and schemes and notebooks and systems for finding balance in my life and for taking care of the necessities of life. This one—a weekly plan with exact and specific activities—has worked the best for me...and for many years. When I came across it, that was *it!* So if you're tired of complicated plans and bulky planners, just keep it simple—eight areas (minimum—you may need additional areas), weekly goals in each area, pared down to which day of the week you'll follow through on each of the activities.

Whatever your system, aim for balance. Managing your life in a wise way will bring sensibility, order, and peace of mind—and balance!—to your life. After all, that's God's high calling here—that we be *sober*-minded, *well*-minded, *sound*-minded, that our passions, thoughts, time, and life be self-controlled. Oh, please, don't give up trying to do well the few things God is calling you to!

Looking Upward

Well, dear one, we already have a lot to think and pray about, don't we? And we've only looked at two of the marks of a woman of wisdom:

> *She knows her priorities...and practices them.*
> *She is balanced in every area of life.*

However, as I'm looking at only these two marks of godly wisdom, they are taking on the glitter and glisten of treasure! What a wonderful surprise—to open up the meaning of just one of God's high callings and discover the gems that can easily turn our lives around! Every woman desires peace and order in her life. Every woman would dearly love to exchange a life of swinging emotions for peace of mind. Every woman would love to exchange failure and frustration for a sure formula for success. Every woman would love to replace a life of survival with a life of meaningful accomplishment. Every woman would love to cash in a life marked by chaos and clutter for a life of priceless order. Every woman would love to trade all of her "oopses" and blunders for a life of wisdom. Every woman would love to give up her out-of-balance, helter-skelter existence for days filled with peace and quiet (in her heart, at least!). And every woman would love to give up the confusion she so easily gives in to for a lifetime characterized by simplicity and stability.

> Wisdom is the God-given ability
> to see life with rare objectivity and
> to handle life with rare stability.[13]

Oh, my precious friend, let this woman of wisdom be you! Let's you and I honor God (and enjoy the treasure that awaits us) by getting our passions under control and nurturing a passion for the very few passions God calls us to. Peace and order and simplicity can be ours...if we will seek to answer God's high calling to walk in wisdom, if we practice our priorities and pursue balance in life's prerequisites.

And now let's look onward...at a few more marks of godly wisdom.

Essential 7

*"...admonish the young women...
to be discreet..."*
—TITUS 2:4-5

*"Wisdom makes it a habit to keep one eye on the
future and the other on reality and makes her
decisions accordingly."*

*"Wisdom weighs all the options and then makes
the right decision."*

*"If any of you lacks wisdom, let him ask of God,
who gives to all liberally and without reproach,
and it will be given to him."*
—JAMES 1:5

Chapter Fourteen

Wisdom—An Essential for Godly Living

I promised you we would come back to the "joke" about the beautiful woman who lacked discretion and wisdom. Do you remember the punch line of this proverb from the Bible? She was like a pig with a gorgeous, expensive ring in its snout—"As a ring of gold in a swine's snout, so is a lovely woman who lacks discretion" (Proverbs 11:22)!

Well, I want to embellish this awful (and ridiculous!) image...and then we'll move on in our continued list of the "Marks of a Woman of Wisdom." To understand this proverb, we must realize that its writer is presenting something that is very incongruous. Each half of the proverb presents something that is a monstrosity, something inappropriate, something hideous and unnatural, something distasteful and offensive, something out-of-place and unbecoming, something ridiculous and absurd. Think about it—a luxurious

197

ornament in the snorting and grubbing snout of a pig! Why, it's as disgusting and ridiculous as...(and the writer continues)...as a physically beautiful woman who lacks good taste, who is disgraceful in her speech and actions, who lacks piety and a well-ordered mind, who is silly, empty, and vulgar. Just like a pig, she is mindless, heartless, shameless, and senseless.

We must make the application—When we as Christian women, women who are supposed to be godly, act without wisdom and discretion, our actions are inconsistent with what others are expecting. And what are they expecting? They are expecting to witness the marks of godliness, the marks of maturity, the marks of a woman of wisdom, of a woman who is serious about answering God's high callings upon her life...and especially His high calling to wisdom.

And now...onward! Let's review and continue on with these exquisite marks of a woman of wisdom.

1. *She knows her priorities...and practices them.*

2. *She is balanced in every area of life.*

3. *She is farsighted*—If I had to say what has meant the most to me in the area of wisdom and discretion, of prudence, sensibility and sober-mindedness, it has been learning about this third important mark of wisdom— that *wisdom is farsighted*. In other words, wisdom makes it a habit to keep one eye on the future and the other on reality and makes her decisions accordingly. In fact, if I had to define wisdom for you, I would say this—

> *Wisdom weighs all the options and then*
> *makes the right decision.*

For instance,

> If I go back to work full time, what will happen to my marriage, my children, our home life, my involvement at the church? (Wisdom takes into consideration wise Solomon's warning that it is ofttimes "the little foxes that spoil the vines"—Song of Solomon 2:15.)

> If I spend our money in this way or on these things...what will happen this month, this year? (Wisdom remembers that the Bible teaches us that riches have wings and so easily fly away—Proverbs 23:5.)

> If I fail to discipline my children now...what will happen later? (Again Proverbs, one of the wisdom books of the Bible, instructs us to discipline our little ones "early," "while there is hope"—Proverbs 13:24 and 19:18.)

> If I waste or spend my time in this way...what will happen to my goals to serve my family and to "build" my home? (I can never get the wisdom from Proverbs out of my head that tells me that "Every wise woman builds her house...and does not eat the bread of idleness"—Proverbs 14:1 and 31:27!)

> If I neglect the disciplines that assist me in taking care of my health...what will that disregard mean in the long run, even later this afternoon? (It's a case of those little foxes again!)

> If I watch or read or listen to this...what will happen to my spiritual growth and my desire to serve the Lord (Proverbs 19:27)?

If I say what I'm thinking...what will happen to the
person who hears it—not to mention the person
it's about? (We know that certain speech "pierces
like a sword" and that the Ultimate Woman of
Wisdom teaches us to open our mouth *only* if
what we are about to say is wise and kind—
Proverbs 12:18 and 31:26.)

I'm sure you're getting the picture, a clear picture of the
importance of each and every decision you and I make. And
I'm also sure you could add your own scenarios and
issues—and scriptures—to the list I've given to start us
thinking about walking in wisdom and discretion. And I'm
praying that you're glimpsing why this essential of wisdom
is so all-important as we seek to follow after God's high callings to godly living.

When it comes to making decisions, I personally try to
keep a clear eye on the potential consequences—good or
bad, favorable or detrimental—of the choices I must (or
might be tempted to) make. I attempt to apply this mark of
maturity (usually, anyway!) to everything—from the food I
put into my mouth to the books I read and put into my
mind, from the way I spend my time to the way I spend
Jim's (eek!) paycheck, from whether I go for an aerobic walk
today...or not...to whether or not I will start up the car today
and go out. Making decisions based on future ramifications
is a challenge (and a discipline), but it's a mark of a woman
who is wise. And that mark, dear one, is a mark we should
covet and pray for...and, with God's help, work for! It's truly
a mark of godliness.

"History" is made every time you make a decision...so you
want to be sure that the decisions you are making clearly
communicate "His story" to others. As Paul wrote to Titus
right here in our passage about God's high calling to His
women, you want to be sure that the life you live is a godly

one that honors and glorifies God rather than dishonors His precious name (Titus 2:5).

So what will it require of you to begin to make decisions that reflect forethought? You're probably already practicing these suggestions, but here's what works for me and for most women I talk to.

- It will require a decision to *pause.* You'll want to distance yourself from the emotions involved in the decisions you must make. The goal is to come to the place in your heart and mind where you can take it or leave it, whatever "it" is. To come to the place where you are passionless in your desires—except in your passion to do what is right, what is best. To come to the place where there's no problem either way—again, you simply want to do what is right! And the first step for gaining a detached attitude (also known as temperance and self-control) is to just simply learn to wait. Don't rush into anything. Make it a habit to wait, even if it's only for a few seconds. Believe it or not, even a few precious split seconds can buy you the opportunity to check your heart, to check in with God, and even to check in with your husband.

- It will require a decision to *pray.* Now, if you (and I!) can conquer the first step—learning to pause and wait, we have a much better chance of *not* making a less-than-wise decision. We also buy time for prayer.

  And what will time in and for prayer accomplish? Through time in prayer you can better gain a neutral heart (Proverbs 14:30). Through time in prayer you can gain wisdom from God (James 1:5). Through time in prayer you can wait on the

Lord (Isaiah 40:31). Through time in prayer you can take care of your own heart (Proverbs 4:23). Through time in prayer you can better make peace with what God's good and acceptable and perfect will is regarding your concern (Philippians 4:6-7). Through time in prayer you can discern God's will regarding the issues surrounding your decision.

• It will require a decision to *ponder*. As we learned earlier, *wisdom weighs all the options and then makes the right decision.* And weighing all the options requires thinking and projecting the results of potential actions and decisions out into the future so that we can get a better picture of the effects a decision might have—both positive and negative, helpful and harmful. That's what the farsightedness and foresight of wisdom is all about. So take the time to ponder!

Three little steps—*pause, pray,* and *ponder.* Oh, my precious reading friend, do you want to be a woman of wisdom? Do you want to live a life that is characterized by peace and joy, by order and meaning? I know I pray daily for this godly mark of maturity in my life! But there's no getting around the fact that a godly life is lived one minute at a time...one thought at a time...one decision at a time. True, one tiny little seemingly harmless decision may not look life-altering, but...

Little choices determine habit;
Habit carves and molds character
Which makes the big decisions.

To make the better and best "little choices" that build in the better and best habits, which sculpt the better and best character, which factors in to the better and best big decisions, you and I must manage our "little choices" wisely.

4. *She works at wisdom*—I love these definitions by writer *par excellence* and teacher Chuck Swindoll that pertain to our subject of wisdom:

> Wisdom is the ability to see with discernment, to view life as God perceives it.
>
> Understanding is the skill to respond with insight.
>
> Knowledge is the rare trait of learning with perception—discovering and growing.[1]

So far in these chapters on wisdom I think (at least, I hope and I pray!) we've addressed the need for discernment. Our definition of wisdom was that "Wisdom weighs all the options and then makes the right decision." That definition (and the wise woman's farsightedness and forethought) seems to embrace discernment. Also we probed our activities, seeking to discern those activities that merely provide you and me with temporary moments of fun and pleasure but fail in the larger field of the eternal. This most definitely encompasses seeking to view life and the variety of activities that can fill the days of our life as God perceives them.

And now, as we study this strong telltale mark of wisdom, we come to Dr. Swindoll's explanation of knowledge as "the rare trait of learning with perception—discovering and growing." Or, as I've stated it, "she works at wisdom."

Several verses in Proverbs, God's treasure book of wisdom, show us what wisdom is and how it's gained. I know we likened the gaining of wisdom to "treasure" in our preceding chapter. And here in Proverbs 2:1-5 (and I've added the emphases), Solomon, acclaimed to be the wisest man in the Old Testament, writes these words (and, by the way, they are a classic example of an "if...then" teaching out of the Bible):

My son,

—*if* you receive my words, and treasure my commands within you, so that you incline your ear to wisdom, and apply your heart to understanding; Yes,

—*if* you cry out for discernment, and lift up your voice for understanding,

—*if* you seek her as silver, and search for her as for hidden treasures;

—*then* you will understand the fear of the LORD, and find the knowledge of God.

In these verses we learn the conditions for receiving the wisdom and knowledge of God—there must be an earnest and sincere seeking of it. Our ears must be open. So must our heart and mind. And our mouths must be crying out for it. And we must work for it, indeed labor for it, as one might work at the digging and mining of silver or hidden treasure. As women pursuing wisdom, our zeal must be in high gear for unearthing *spiritual* riches rather than *material* riches. As the writer of Proverbs said elsewhere, "Wisdom is the principal thing; therefore get wisdom. And in all your getting, get understanding" (Proverbs 4:7).

So, what are some things we can do to extract God's precious treasure of wisdom? How exactly can we discover and grow in wisdom and knowledge? How can we become wise?

Spiritually...we must pray for wisdom. As Proverbs 2:3 stated, we must cry out for wisdom, appeal to God for it. James as much as said the same thing when he wrote, "If any of you lacks wisdom, let him ask of God..." (James 1:5). And we must familiarize ourselves with the Word of God, for indeed, His Word *is* His wisdom, written for all times. One verse I cling to for living in these "changing" times is Psalm 33:11, "The counsel of the LORD stands forever, the plans of His heart to all generations." And I would also say take time to master the book of Proverbs, a truly inspired book of timeless truth and wisdom.

Mentally...purposefully take time to think, plan, schedule, and prepare for each day or each event in your life. Yet another proverb teaches us that "the preparations of the heart belong to man" (Proverbs 16:1). The language here speaks of placing things in order, of setting a battle array, of laying a fire. Each is done carefully and with thought. This, dear one, is how we as women of wisdom are to approach each precious day. We must prepare for it and plan for it, which requires time, thought, and prayer. (And, of course, as this proverb also reminds us, the final outcome is from God. God always accomplishes His purposes!)

Practically...follow through on your plans and your schedule. It's one thing to plan and make a schedule (which is usually done sitting down!). It's quite another to act on those plans (which usually requires getting up and doing something!). But once she has prayed over her day and her life and pinpointed the very few important things that must be done to keep her life and family on God's track, then the wise woman follows through...with gusto! After all, "In all labor there is profit, but idle chatter leads only to poverty" (Proverbs 14:23)! In other words, thinking and praying and planning and talking about work is one thing—doing it is quite another!

Educationally...Be wise and ask other women about this matter of godly wisdom. Actively seek out those with more experience, those who demonstrate this wonderful, admirable character quality. That's what Titus 2:3-5 is all about—our sisterhood with other women of God. We are a family with an assignment to help one another. Our older sisters are to instruct, and our younger sisters are to ask and seek to learn. And, as we've stressed throughout this book, *we are both*—both the older woman who is always to be teaching someone else and the younger woman who is always to be learning from someone else.

5. *She practices the seven steps of wisdom*—One day many years ago, in an overly ambitious move on my part, I decided to begin an in-depth study of the book of Proverbs. As you can probably tell, these pithy sayings are a passion of mine and have been a personal project for a good quarter-century. Well, I can't exactly tell you how far I've gotten on that study, nor how many times that rich pursuit has been halted and started all over again.

But...on the very first day of my study, in the very first chapter of Proverbs, I "stumbled" across what I have since adopted as my "Seven Steps of Wisdom." The picture Solomon paints in portions of Proverbs 1 is one of a full-of-energy young man charging into life. With all his vigor, this youth is instructed to give attention to caution and to gaining wisdom, instruction, prudence, and discretion...*before* decisions are made and actions are taken. As I said, my study led me to formulate these Seven Steps of Wisdom for my own life:

Seven Steps of Wisdom
Step 1—Stop
Step 2—Wait
Step 3—Pray
Step 4—Search the Scriptures
Step 5—Ask for wise counsel
Step 6—Make a decision
Step 7—Create a plan

My dear friend, I cannot begin to tell you how valuable these steps have been to me over the years! It's impossible to count how many times they have saved me from sinning, from stumbling, or from making a foolish decision or statement! They have served me well, and also the many women I've shared them with over the years. They suffice for the smallest decisions right on up the scale to the earth-shattering, life-changing ones!

Let me tell you about my most recent use of these simple seven steps of wisdom. This past weekend I was trying to give a message on the fruit of the Spirit at a nearby hotel here in California. The women had done a lovely job of planning and praying and organizing their retreat. However, no one knew that a high school prom—complete with a band and a disc jockey—was scheduled to occur in the ballroom next to our meeting room, right on the other side of a cloth partition.

When we began our session, all was quiet, but about 20 minutes into our meeting the band started up. I mean, it was an impossible situation! So what did I do?

I *stopped*...at least in my heart before I did anything like stop my message, give up, or walk off.

I *waited*...to see what would happen (would those in the next room respond to the coordinator's plea? Would they turn down the volume enough so that we could function? Would the coordinator walk up and stop the session herself?)

I *prayed*...yes, I was still talking to the women, but believe me, I was also talking to the Lord!

I *searched the Scriptures* (in my heart and mind, at least!)... and a plethora of memory verses raced through my brain as I stood there and continued to teach and at the same time prayed for wisdom. I begged God for something from His Word to guide me. The scriptures that came to mind ranged from "Greater is He who is in you [God] than he that is in the world [Satan]" to Jesus' words to His disciples to the effect that "I have much to say to you but you are not able to *hear* it!!!!!"

I *asked for wise counsel*...by looking to my husband Jim who was standing outside the door making a sign (a swiping motion across his throat) that clearly said "kill it," "cut it," "stop it!" Anyway, I got the message!

I *made a decision*...to stop.

I *created a plan* to execute my decision...I explained that I was stopping and issued a promise to review what had been shared the next morning.

And I want you to know, dear reader, that afterwards, the decision and the process was affirmed 100 percent (even 1000 percent!) by the leaders, by the women in attendance, by my husband, and even by the hotel staff. (And just an added word—that's usually the way it is with true wisdom. As James puts it, "the wisdom that is from above is first pure, then peaceable, gentle, willing to yield, full of mercy and good fruits, without partiality and without hypocrisy" (James 3:17).

My advice to you? Memorize these seven steps and begin applying them to not only the tiniest decisions but right on up to the biggest decisions. And remember, sometimes the process is completed in a matter of seconds or minutes, as was mine in the scenario above. And sometimes it may take weeks or months as you work your way through (and up) these practical steps. Don't be afraid to wait a long time, to pray for weeks, even to fast, to meet with a counselor for months...until God gives you the wisdom that is His.

Looking Upward

As a book *about* wisdom and a book *of* wisdom, Proverbs never fails to show us what wisdom is and what wisdom does. But the book of Proverbs also shows us the *source* of wisdom and *how* to attain this precious and priceless "principal thing" (Proverbs 4:7). What is the *source* of wisdom? And *how* do we attain it? Hear the Word of the Lord:

> The fear of the LORD is the beginning of wisdom, and
> the knowledge of the Holy One is understanding.
> (Proverbs 9:10)

The level of our love for God and His Word determines if we will be wise or not. We either fear and revere Him or we don't. We either seek His direction or we don't. God *is* wisdom, and God *is* knowledge. When we look upward—to Him and to His Word, and when we desire Him—His wisdom and His ways, then, dear one, our lives will bear the rare and beautiful marks of wisdom, and we will act with discretion. We will choose to live life according to the high callings and the priorities God sets down for us as His women.

Essential 8

"...admonish the young women...to be chaste..."
—TITUS 2:4-5

"Do you want to be a godly woman? Then heed two never-changing essentials for godly living—Keep yourself pure in body, and keep yourself pure in mind."

"We are to be modest, immaculate, and pure from immorality. Therefore, may our pure soul look upward, mount up on wings and cut a path into the heaven of glory, leaving a track of light for men to wonder at!"

"Blessed are the pure in heart, for they shall see God."
—MATTHEW 5:8

Chapter Fifteen

A Woman's High Calling to Purity

ecently I had a shocking experience. I shouldn't have been shocked. But I was. I've attended quite a few retreats as a Christian woman. And I've always enjoyed the "sharing" times at the close of such events. The women generally tell about something they've learned from the Word of God during the course of the weekend.

But...this particular time was different. It all began with a woman still in her teens—her late teens (19) who shared that she had "lost her virginity" during the past year. She told of her shame and her disappointment, in herself and in her first experience with sex. (You see, it was nowhere near what she'd been told it would be! Isn't that so like Satan's lies?!)

Well, I wasn't prepared for the dam that then broke open as teen after teen and then married woman after married woman related similar stories, some of experimentation with sex before marriage and some after and during!

As I think back upon the pain in my own heart at hearing such an outpouring of remorse and regret, shame and guilt, I believe that perhaps *sobered* is a better word than *shocked* to describe my overall response. Just think about it! The lack of purity. The broken vows. The broken hearts. The broken lives. Yes, God forgives those who repent. Indeed, He washes such "scarlet" sins "as white as snow" (Isaiah 1:18). But there are always consequences...such as the women related...so that, no matter how many years had passed, not a day went by that they did not remember their loss and feel their remorse. As the meeting drew to a close, the teens spent their last minutes pleading with the other women— the older women, the teachers, and the mothers—to warn their daughters and the young teens in their church to preserve their purity.

In the end, another teen, through tears and sobs, shared about her friend whose mother and father gave her a bolt of white satin fabric and a strand of white pearls on her twelfth birthday. These wise parents told their precious and much-loved preteen daughter that "if she didn't smoke or drink or take drugs or have sex before she married, God would richly reward her." Gulping between sobs, the girl who was telling this story lamented that her parents had never seemed to care about these things. With anguish, she shared how she wished they had cared enough to do something like that for her, and how she hoped the moms in the audience would do something like that for their daughters.

As I said, it was quite sobering...and eye-opening. You and I must not only take seriously our own high calling to purity, but also, as our passage from Titus 2:3-5 is teaching us, our responsibility as women who are older than *any* other woman—even teens, even *preteens*!—to teach and admonish others (starting with our very own daughters) in this all-important high calling to chasteness and purity. May this haunting reminder serve us as a wake-up call!

Purity As a Calling

You and I, my dear faithful reading companion, are heading toward the end of our wonderful, inspiring (hopefully!), challenging, and motivating (again, I hope and pray!) study of ten high callings from God upon our lives as women. I know I've certainly been "sobered" and reminded of what it is God wants us to *be* for Him and to *do* for Him as we've probed the ten essentials God lists in Titus 2:3-5 for living our lives in a godly manner that brings glory to Him (verse 5). So far...

> ...we've looked at the virtues the older women are to nurture in Christ through their years of walking with Him in obedience—what God wants us to *be*.

> ...we've considered, too, the first half of the curriculum the older women are called by God to teach to their younger sisters in the body of Christ—beginning with how to love their husband and their children—what God wants us to *do*. The first two subjects on this list of divine coursework have to do with marriage and family, with family relationships, with being a loving wife and mother...no matter what kind of husband or child dwells under our roof. As one scholar writes, our "first duty is to make home life attractive and beautiful by love of husband and children."[1]

> ...we've also examined our calling from God to a "must" for every Christian—to walk in

wisdom and discretion and self-control, character qualities that are reflected in sober-mindedness in all things.

And now, the apostle Paul writes to "Pastor Titus"—and
to us—that the older women are to teach the young women
to be chaste (Titus 2:4-5). This is yet another calling to personal character, to moral purity, to sexual purity, and to marital faithfulness.[2] And, dear one, it is essential!

Purity Defined

I think most of us have some idea of what pure means
(referred to as "chaste" in the King James Version of the
Bible). English definitions describe *pure* as being without
stain or taint, being free from pollution, having cleanliness,
being innocent and guiltless.

In our New Testament, the Greek word Paul used in Titus
2:5 for "pure" is *hagnos*. It is used...

...one time for *chaste* (1 Peter 3:2—husbands are to
witness chaste conduct in their wives)
...one time for *free from sin* (1 Timothy 5:22—elders
are to keep themselves from sin, as purity is
a mark of maturity)
...one time for *innocent* (2 Corinthians 7:11—the
godly sorrow of the Corinthians over sin
proved them to be innocent and cleared from
every stain of guilt for that sin)
...five times for *pure*
—We are to be as pure and as chaste as a virgin
(2 Corinthians 11:2).
—We are to think pure thoughts (Philippians 4:8).
—We are to learn to be chaste and pure in all our
actions and in all our relationships (Titus 2:5).

—We are to seek wisdom that is pure and godly
(James 3:17).

—We are to purify ourselves from all known sin
(1 John 3:3).

All summed up, you and I are to first look to God for His divine enablement and grace… and then do all we can to be pure, pure-minded, and pure from immorality. We are to actively seek to answer God's high calling to purity. For, indeed, that's what godliness is!

How can I say that? Read on… .

Purity Explained

The Greek word Paul used in Titus 2:5 for "pure" is *hagnos*, which comes from *hagios*. When we realize that *hagios* is used in the New Testament for *Holy, Holy of Holies*, and *Holy one*, we begin to grasp the fact that there is a much heavier and weightier meaning for "purity" than we generally ascribe to it in our morally-lax times.

Initially *pure* meant that a person had gone through the ritualistic cleansings required by the Mosaic law prior to worship. But as time went on, *pure* came to describe the moral purity that alone can approach the gods. It's been reported that "on the Temple of Aesculapius at Epidaurus there was the inscription at the entrance: 'He who would enter the divine temple must be pure *(hagnos);* and purity is to have a mind which thinks holy thoughts.'" In other words, to be *pure* means to be so cleansed of all ulterior motives and of self that one has become *pure* enough to see God. Rather than wishing to escape God's sight; the one who is *pure* is able to bear His very scrutiny.[3]

So (and I hope you're still following along!), in Titus 2:4-5 God calls the young women to live a godly life of *purity*. They are to love their husbands and children. And they are to be wise and discreet in their behavior. And *purity* helps explain what kind of wisdom and discretion and self-control the young women needed in order to properly love their husbands—they were to control their passions and desires and remain true to their husbands.[4]

Purity…and the Lack Thereof! *…Demonstrated*

We don't have to look very far in our Bible to find models of women whose conduct was godly, pristine, and pure. Sadly, we also find examples of women whose behavior was anything but pure. Let's look first at a few unfavorable or negative models. Then we'll move on to something purer and more positive, to admiring several women who brilliantly demonstrated purity for us.

Dinah—This poor woman's story is detailed in Genesis 34. Dinah had everything going for her. She was the daughter of the patriarch Jacob and his wife Leah. However, the Bible text reports that Dinah "went out to see the daughters of the land" (Genesis 34:1). Evidently, Dinah left the safety of her family quarters and ventured outside to take a look at the land and to visit with the local women. However, "when Shechem the son of Hamor the Hivite, prince of the country, saw her, he took her and lay with her, and violated her" (verse 2). Bad went to worse as Dinah's brothers took the matter of retribution into their own hands and maliciously connived to murder all the males of the Hivite camp.

And, dear reader, that is the end of this woman-full-of-promise's biography. Dinah "slipped back into oblivion," shamed and forgotten, and was never mentioned again. Someone well described Dinah's tale as "Dinah's sad moment in the spotlight."[5] Her curiosity and failure to use good wisdom contributed to her defilement. One scholar describes the scene in this way (sending us as women who desire to live godly lives a loud message to *stay home!*):

> Dinah's love for sight-seeing set off a train of tragic consequences. Young and daring, and curious to know something of the world outside, she stole away one day from the drab tents of her father, to see how the girls in their gorgeous Oriental trappings fared in nearby Shechem. Roaming around, the eyes of Prince Shechem...lighted upon her....Had Dinah been content to remain a "keeper at home" (Titus 2:5), a terrible [thing] would have been averted, but her desire for novelty and forbidden company spelled disaster.[6]

Potiphar's wife—While poor Dinah fell victim to the lusts and desires of another, the story of Potiphar's wife, on the other hand, shows us a woman who, driven by her own lusts and desires, victimized another. We read of her bold and blatant advances toward the innocent and godly Joseph in Genesis 39. As the faithful overseer of his master Potiphar's household, Joseph took care of all the needs of both the people and the place under Potiphar's roof. However, we learn that Potiphar's wife "cast longing eyes on Joseph, and she said, 'Lie with me'" (Genesis 39:7).

And what was Joseph's reply? In a word, No! And the Bible reports that this scenario went on day after day after day (verse 10). Finally Potiphar's wife literally and physically grabbed Joseph, who fled from his master's wife's grasp so quickly that his garment was left in her hand.

And what was the result of one immoral woman's lack of decency and virtue? Of her thinking only of what she wanted? Of her scheming to get what she craved? Joseph, a man of integrity, a pure man who was innocent and unjustly accused, was put in prison for possibly two to three years. You see, when we dwell on ourselves and what we want, and when we fail to hold our thoughts and passions in check (along with failing to think of others!), others get hurt... and so do we. And, worst of all, God is dishonored (Titus 2:5).

Hear these challenging words to us regarding the thoughts we think...and the harm they can—and will—ultimately cause:

> Are you harboring lustful thoughts? Do you excuse it because you think no one knows and no one will get hurt? Polluting your thoughts and desires *will* eventually hurt the people in your life whom you say you love. If you are ensnared in a habit of lust...God can heal you and give you a new life. Seek help from a caring church. Impure thoughts are not harmless thoughts.[7]

Oh, dear friend, as this same writer so succinctly puts it,

"Sin is spelled **S**-e-l-f-**I**-s-h-**N**-e-s-s"![8]

Are you sobered? Are your eyes wide open? Are you more aware now of how a failure to guard your thoughts and actions—a failure to keep them pure—can lead to personal ruin and to the ruin of others? I know I am! Dinah and Potiphar's wife teach us many lessons in wisdom and on the need and responsibility we as women must recognize is ours in this vital area of purity.

But there's more to glean from more women of the Bible. This time let's look at a few of the "good" ones!

Ruth—What a lady! As a Moabitess, this heathen woman learned about the true God from her husband's family. However, Ruth was a widow now. But she pledged her undying loyalty to her widowed mother-in-law Naomi with these famous words, "Your people shall be my people, and your God, my God" (Ruth 1:16).

As the Lord so sovereignly arranged it, a kinsman named Boaz entered Ruth's life. And, in the custom of the day, Ruth revealed to Boaz her desire to marry him by lying at his feet all night (see Ruth 3:7-14). Yet even as she lay at his feet throughout the night, Ruth's godliness and purity and excellence of character shone brilliantly in the dark night. So brilliantly, in fact, that Boaz declared, "All the people of my town know that you are a virtuous woman" (verse 11).

May our reputation ever be as pure...and praiseworthy!

Mary—And, speaking of purity and excellence of character, perhaps no woman in the Bible shines as brilliantly as does Mary, the mother of our Lord Jesus. This young woman was spoken of as a "highly favored one," as a woman who "found favor with God" (Luke 1:28,30).

And exactly what had Mary, possibly a fourteen-year-old, a teenager, done to be addressed in this way by God's magnificent angelic messenger Gabriel? We know several things:

> *First*, Mary was a virgin. She had kept herself pure. Gabriel was sent "to a virgin...and that virgin's name was Mary" (verse 27). As she asked the mighty angel for clarification after he announced that she would conceive a baby, Mary herself said, "How can this be, since I do not know a man?" (verse 34). But, because she was a virgin and because she had found favor with God, she was "blessed...among women" (verse 42) to be the mother of Jesus. Mary's purity and virginity were crucially important to Jesus' being virgin-born, authenticating His deity and sinlessness.
>
> *Second*, Mary's heart and mind were filled with the Word of the Lord. As this young woman burst into praise to God in what is known as the "Magnificat" in Luke 1:46-55, her heart and mind were

revealed by her words. And what do we learn from her utterances? Hers was a soul riveted on the Lord, on the Word of God, on the psalms, on the law, and on the prophets. Indeed, her Magnificat is filled with Old Testament quotations and references. Here was a youthful virgin who appears not only to have been pure in body but also pure in mind—one whose mind truly dwelt on things above (Colossians 3:2).

Do you want to be a godly woman? Then look at the life of Mary, which shows us two never-changing ways—two essentials for godly living: Keep yourself *pure in body,* and keep yourself *pure in mind* (1 Corinthians 7:34).

Elizabeth—I can't resist adding this dear woman and hero of mine to our list of women who took God's high calling to purity seriously! Elizabeth's story doesn't point so much to sexual and moral purity as it does to her thought life and spiritual worship and pure heart. Like her cousin Mary, Elizabeth loved the Lord in thought, word, and deed.

And like most of the women of the Bible, Elizabeth had a problem. In her case, she was married but she was barren and also well advanced in years (Luke 1:7). Humanly speaking, Elizabeth was never going to have a baby.

But the thing I love most about Elizabeth is that she didn't allow her predicament to affect her love and devotion to God. For, as Luke explains, she and her husband "were both righteous before God, walking in all the commandments and ordinances of the Lord blameless" (verse 6). In spite of the heartbreak and social stigma of barrenness, Elizabeth and her husband obeyed God's law and fulfilled all His commandments and ordinances. They were most definitely ceremonially *pure.* But I believe they were also *pure in heart.* They looked upward to the Lord, they prayed (verse 13), and they went on to serve Him, her husband as a priest and Elizabeth as his faithful-though-childless wife.

And then blessing-of-all-blessings(!), Gabriel, an angel of the Lord, appeared to Elizabeth's husband Zacharias while he was serving in the temple of the Lord. And what was the purpose of this divine being's miraculous appearing? Gabriel was sent from the very presence of God (verse 19) to let Zacharias and Elizabeth know that they would have a son, whom they were to name John (verse 13). This son would to be John the Baptist, the forerunner of Jesus Christ the Messiah (verse 13-17).

In the end, Elizabeth was blessed to become a mother— and of a very special little boy! Yet nothing deterred Elizabeth's passion for God and for being a godly woman. Not barrenness. Not her public "reproach" (Luke 1:25). Not the bleak future prospect of a lack of babies to love and heirs to carry on the family line. No, Elizabeth brings to us a portrait of unusual piety, strong faith, and an unfeigned devotion to God that was not based upon her personal situation. She was one who set about to answer God's high calling... no matter what!

Looking Upward

My dear sister-in-pursuit-of-godliness, our high calling to purity is vital! It is vital to our own godliness (Titus 2:3). It is vital in our relationships with men (verse 5). It is vital that we teach it to others (verses 3 and 4). And it is vital to the cause and reputation of God (verse 5).

Indeed, we are to be modest, immaculate, and pure from immorality. Therefore, beloved sister-in-Christ, may your pure soul look upward, mount up on wings and cut a path into the heaven of glory, leaving a track of light for men to wonder at![9]

Essential

"...admonish the young women...to be chaste..."
—TITUS 2:4-5

"When the fervency of our heart for God slips from hot to lukewarm or cold, our actions and choices will reflect that temperature change. It's a given! Our solution, then, is the heart, because 'only a passionate love of purity can save a woman from impurity.' So pray for a passionate heart for purity!"

"Every deed calls for purity when we are seeking to glorify God with our every act."

"What can we do to nurture greater purity? We must think on whatever things are pure. We must 'seek those things which are above where Christ is' and set our minds on things above, not on things on the earth."

Chapter Sixteen

Purity—An Essential for Godly Living

I began our last chapter with something shocking (at least to me). And now, my friend, I want to do the same again here with a few statements and words of explanation about the importance of purity from Dr. Gene Getz, a former professor at Dallas Theological Seminary. Dr. Getz writes these words: "The subjects emphasized by biblical writers reflect the major problems in New Testament churches, and no problem is dealt with more consistently than immorality. Hardly a letter was penned that did not treat this subject specifically, graphically, and with candor." Then, in his classic book, *The Measure of a Woman*, Getz continues, "Paul was concerned that *all* Christian women, young and old alike, realize their responsibility in maintaining pure relationships with men....History is filled with accounts of men who, though rulers over kingdoms and people, were often

under the spell of beautiful and sensual women."[1] Put
another way, the number one problem in the churches in the
days of Paul and Titus was immorality. And most will agree
that the number one problem in the church today is still
immorality.

I don't know what you're thinking right this minute, but
these statements comprise a serious "call" to purity and
careful conduct. And that is exactly what Paul is asking of
you and me in Titus 2:3-5. Our high calling, whether we're
in that special category of "older women" (verse 3) or
whether we consider ourselves to be in the "young women"
group (verse 4), is to be reverent and holy in behavior,
chaste and pure (verses 3 and 5).

As we move into this practical section, let's begin with
this "checklist" for purity.

✓ *Purity is an issue of the heart*—Behavior is determined by where the heart is set. In Proverbs 2:17
   an adulterous wife and woman is described as
   one who has forgotten "the covenant of her
   God." Marriage vows are made before God and in
   His presence. And God's seventh commandment
   prohibits adultery. Therefore, the woman who
   commits adultery is a woman whose heart is no
   longer set on the Lord her God nor on His standards for godly living. The same is surely true of
   any and all acts that signal a wandering away
   from those things that please and honor God.
   When the fervency of our heart for God slips
   from hot to lukewarm or cold, our actions and
   choices will reflect that temperature change. It's a
   given! Our solution, then, is the heart. And, as
   one has written, "Only a passionate love of purity
   can save a man [or a woman] from impurity."[2] So,
   dear one, pray for a passionate heart for purity!

✓ *Purity is an issue of character*—Purity is related to personal character. Therefore, the woman who is chaste and pure at the core will manifest purity in thought, word, and deed by a habitual self-restraint which gives no ground for evil reports.[3]

✓ *Purity is an issue of the mind*—The world is full of things that are sordid and shabby and soiled and smutty. And if we're not alert, on guard, and careful, our thoughts can soil our soul and taint everything we think and do. The goal of every Christian woman should be to set her mind on the things which are pure (Philippians 4:8).

✓ *Purity is an issue of modesty*—Eventually our character and our thoughts show up in our behavior, conduct, dress, manner, speech, and body language. And, even in these everyday externals, we as representatives of a thrice-holy God, as His wives and mothers and as members of His church, are to be modest, chaste and pure, reserved and proper.

Obviously, purity is an area—indeed, a high calling!—where we women are to practice great wisdom and discretion and self-control. It's essential!

And now...for some "Yes, but how?" suggestions!

How Can We Be Pure in Thought?

A few "no's" and "not's" will help us out here.

1. *Use the word No!*—It's been pointed out many times and in many places that the key to chasteness and purity is the little two-letter word No! So, my friend, you and I have got to say No! to all

thoughts about any man other than our own husbands. That's the context here of Paul's instruction to Titus to have the older women teach the younger *wives* to major on purity and chasteness in their marriages. And it's true, just as Jesus warned us, that "from within, out of the heart of men, proceed evil thoughts, adulteries, fornications..." (Mark 7:21).

Therefore, to answer God's high calling to stay pure in mind means thinking no thoughts that might even cause you to fantasize about any other man, real or imaginary! It means saying No! to anything you might see or read that could plant any such impure thoughts in your mind. Don't even allow your mind to flit across these destructive ideas.

And watch out! Watch out for what you watch—soap operas, mini-series, movies, talk shows, even documentaries and interviews—that parade and applaud such acts and the people who commit them. Watch out, too, for the philosophy of magazines on the newsstands. As the Bible cautions us, "Beware lest anyone cheat [or 'spoil'—KJV] you through philosophy and empty deceit, according to the tradition of men, according to the basic principles of the world, and not according to Christ" (Colossians 2:8).

2. *Develop a battle plan*—What can we do to nurture greater purity? We must mount a counter-offense! We must go to battle! We must *think* on whatever things are pure (Philippians 4:8). We must *seek* those things which are above where Christ is and *set* our minds on things above, not on things on the earth (Colossians 3:1-2). We must do as David did and *write out* "A Vow for a Holy Life."[4] Hear

these words drawn from David's vow in Psalm 101:1-4:

A Vow for a Holy Life

I will sing praises.
I will behave wisely in a perfect way.
I will walk within my house with a perfect heart.
I will set nothing wicked before my eyes.
I will not know wickedness.

—from Psalm 101:1-4

3. *Feed on the Word of God*—As you and I desire the purity God desires for us, we must keep our head in the Word of God…and the Word of God in our head. We must feed on it, read it, memorize it, meditate on it, study it, cherish it, lean on it, and live by it. These words in the Psalms tell us of the powerful impact God's Word can have on our life…and our heart: "Your word I have hidden in my heart, that I might not sin against You" (Psalm 119:11).

4. *Make a radical commitment*—We must be radical about our purity. What might that mean? It means staying away (as much as is possible) from people who talk explicitly about sex. It means cutting things out of your life—things like we mentioned above. It means eradicating any behaviors that cause problems for you or for men. Don't be afraid to be radical about your purity. As someone has said, "Saying 'yes' to God means saying 'no' to

things which offend His holiness." And I would add...saying "no" to things which offend others.

How Can We Be Pure in Word?

Whether we acknowledge it or not, what we allow our-self to think will...sooner or later...be expressed by our words. Thoughts lead to words. It's just as Jesus said— "...out of the abundance of the heart the mouth speaks" (Matthew 12:34).

It's hard for me to write these things, but I've decided that if I can ask these questions of myself, then perhaps they will help you, too. So here goes...

What are your favorite topics of conversation?

What do you tend to talk about?

Do you use sexual slang words or words with double meanings?

Do you share off-color jokes and stories?

Do you laugh along with others when they do?

Do you discuss your sex life...or listen to others dis-cuss theirs?

Do you pass on accounts of sexual problems another person has shared?

And please, I'm not talking about counseling situations. That's different, although such sharing should always be handled carefully and discreetly. There are issues in a mar-ried woman's life that sometimes require counsel. And this is exactly the point of this passage from Titus 2:3-5. Paul told Titus to tell the older women to teach and instruct the younger women in how to love their husband and to be chaste. That's the older woman's duty, her ministry, her assignment from God. So by all means, look to those godly women—who do not gossip (Titus 2:3!)—who can help you.

Also be aware and careful of your speech when you are around men other than your husband. For instance, Dr. Gene Getz advises that we women should avoid using endearing terms around men, such as calling men "love," "dear," "sweetie," "precious," "sugar," etc.[5] (And remember—this counsel is coming from a *man!*)

Another potential for causing a man to stumble (which reveals our lack of purity) is complimenting men other than your husband on their looks, clothing, physique, body, or masculinity.

And there's still another off-limits area in this vital area of speech—don't discuss with another man controversial sexual issues. Once you've discussed such items with a man, you've crossed a line of intimacy!

How Can We Be Pure in Deed?

Every deed calls for purity when we are seeking to glorify God with our *every* act. The list of ways and decisions we must make regarding our actions is endless. However, there is one decision we face at least once every day, and that is the age-old decision of "What should I wear today?" Our choice of clothing, which is a deed in itself, is a day-in, day-out challenge in the area of purity. As women desiring to answer God's high calling, we should wonder what God says about what we should wear. What guidelines does He in His Word offer us? Read the following scriptures:

> *I desire…that the women adorn themselves*
> *in modest apparel, with propriety and moderation…*
> *which is proper for women professing*
> *godliness, with good works.*
> (1 Timothy 2:8-10)

Note the three clear guidelines found in these verses for choosing our attire. When these three "guidelines for godly grooming" are applied each time we approach the closet, what we wear will reflect the beauty and order—and purity!—of the Lord and our love for Him.

> Guideline #1—*modesty*. This may seem like a prudish and outdated word (especially in our lax and lacking-standards-world!), but it's a term from the Bible. Modesty is a wonderful word that helps us understand God's high calling to purity. This singular word, meaning orderly, wraps its arms around all that is proper, appropriate, tasteful, and befitting of a woman who is called by God to godliness, holiness, and purity (Titus 2:3,5).

> Guideline #2—*propriety*. Our dress should reflect our deep reverence for the God we love. He is holy, and our clothing should send forth a message about that holiness, indicating a woman who is concerned with inner purity, a woman who is set apart in heart to the Lord. Our God is worthy of respect, so shouldn't our clothing invite the respect of others, rather than their stares, shock, or scorn?

> Guideline #3—*moderation*. Our calling as a daughter of the King is a serious calling, so our attire should indicate the seriousness with which we regard our privileged position in Christ. Our dress is to reveal a refined moderation to signal that we are women of self-restraint and discretion.

And now I have a sad story to share, which brought a large lesson home to me. While I was in Israel on a visit to the Holy Land with a group of other Christians, I was embarrassed when the Muslims who tended the entrances of many religious sites in Jerusalem would not allow some of our women into their places of worship. Why? Because we had violated their standards for modesty in women. They required that those who entered their mosques dress more modestly than some on our Christian tour group were dressed. What were some of their problems with our assembly of ladies? Bare shoulders, tops with spaghetti straps, form fitting tops, bare midriffs, shorts revealing "too much" leg. On and on their list went...and we were guilty on every offense! These heathen unbelievers had a higher standard for women in general, for women, period, than we had as women who should be seeking to be godly in heart, soul, behavior...and appearance. In the end, we had not only violated the standards these Arabs had set, but the standards *God* has set for His women—women who are to be godly and holy and pure and chaste, women who are to dress with modesty, with propriety, and with moderation.

A Picture of Impurity

As I wrote earlier, it's been hard for me to write about the specifics of purity. But it is my deep desire to help women like you and me along the path toward greater purity! And again...it's our high calling. And it's essential!

But now I want to take a paragraph or two and let God show us some of the specifics of *impurity!* He spares no details as He vividly paints a picture for us of an adulterous woman in Proverbs 7. First read Proverbs 7—all of it!—in your own Bible and then take a look at a list of this awful, depraved, licentious woman's thoughts, words, and deeds.

Proverbs 7—A Portrait of an Adulterous Woman

Her night appearance (verse 10)—she appeared at night...and alone, something females in this woman's day never did!

Her dress (verse 10)—she was garishly and conspicuously attired, marked out as "different."

Her voice (verse 11)—she was loud and boisterous, clamoring for attention (a reference to an animal in heat).

Her character (verse 11)—she was stubborn and rebellious and restless (another reference to an animal that refuses to receive a bridle).

Her feet (verse 11)—rather than being at home, she is "out there."

Her methods (verse 13)—she physically and aggressively attacks the man and kisses him.

Her words (verse 14)—her words are deceptive as she refers to food obtained from a sacrifice to God, and sensual and inviting as she speaks of hunger. Then she moves to flattery (verse 15) and more sensuality as she describes her bedroom, her bed, her bed linens, aromatic spices, and the satisfaction of sexual desires (verses 16-18)!

Truly, one picture is worth a thousand words! Just count the many ways this woman broke all the rules of purity, indicators of impure thoughts leading to impure words leading to impure deeds! May we steer completely clear of any such manners and methods! And may we never cease to steer our daughters clear of the same. As godly moms, we are to train up our girls in the way they should go—in God's way and the way of the godly woman!

Looking Upward

As was said at the beginning of this chapter, immorality is a major issue in the church, if not *the* major issue. Obviously our society is becoming more and more corrupt and immoral. What were once considered "off-limit" practices even ten years ago seem to be commonplace today. And, if we as holy sisters-in-Christ are not careful, the same low standards just might affect us...and our daughters! Impurity is a real threat and a sobering issue.

How can we as Christian women stop this downward slide? We stop it, first, at our own heart's doorstep...by thinking on what is pure, by guarding our heart more than any treasure, and by loving the Lord with all our heart, soul, strength, and mind. We stop it, also, at our home's doorstep. We are called to be the watch-women (Proverbs 31:27) who are to guard our household against a declining morality. We are to be ever vigilant against all that does not meet our holy God's holy standard! May we, like David, walk within our house with a perfect heart and set nothing wicked before our eyes and the eyes of our family!

Oh, dear one, let's give much prayer (and action!) to these few practical ways to ensure our own purity as we look upward to God and to His divine, dazzling thrice-holy purity.

Acknowledge God's standard.
Assume God's standard as your standard.
Admit any and all sin against God's standard.
Avoid compromising situations.
Avoid compromising people.
Ask for accountability.
Acknowledge the consequences impurity reaps.
Aspire to a life of obedience—a holy life has a
  voice!

Essential

"...admonish the young women...
to be homemakers..."
—TITUS 2:4-5

"If our home is a ministry, shouldn't that min-
istry become a passion? Shouldn't our feelings
and emotions be involved when it comes to the
people and place we love? And shouldn't our
work be done passionately? Shouldn't our labors
be labors of love?"

"Every wise woman builds her house."
—PROVERBS 14:1

"When we get up every morning with a fresh
prayer for our home in our heart, and a burning
passion for building our home in our soul, when
we acknowledge the priority, and pledge to better
the lives of the people at home by bettering the
place of home, and then practice the many tasks
that such love requires, in time we master the
skills of homemaking."

Chapter Seventeen

A Woman's High Calling to Her Home

During the twenty-plus years when my daughter Courtney was growing up, she loved to help me in the kitchen with the cooking and baking of our meals and goodies. In fact, one of my favorite pictures of Courtney is of her as a toddler wearing her little apron, standing on a kitchen chair so she could be counter-height and help "cook." Yes, she's always enjoyed working in the kitchen!

And Courtney's passion further blossomed when she married and set up her own home. She continued to nurture her interest in food preparation while she and her Paul moved around due to Paul's career as a teacher and during his years of earning a graduate degree. No matter where the Lord took Courtney and Paul, she served food fit for kings to her Paul and the many students, family members, church people, and friends who were blessed to visit them and partake of her fancy for cooking!

Early one morning Jim and I received a call from Courtney. She and Paul had decided that while he was finishing up his master's degree at Colorado State University, she should take advantage of some night classes being offered at a famous culinary school in the area on the evenings when Paul had his classes. Oh, was she ever excited! And so were we! What a good thing to do with her time and talent (rather than sulking, moping, pining away in loneliness and self-pity...or over-indulging in TV)! Jim and I could hardly wait to hear her report of the fine fruits of that first culinary class. We could only imagine all the grand dishes she would concoct that inaugural evening. It was D-Day!

Well, sure enough, the next morning she called to tell us all about her plunge into the culinary arts! But, my dear reading friend, I have to report to you that the report was *not* what we anticipated! No, to our surprise, Courtney's first class had been completely dedicated to one skill, one exercise, one task—chopping! She had spent her first four-hour class learning how important it is to choose the right kind of knife and learn how to chop foods in preparation for cooking! (Did you know that there is a right way and a wrong way to chop?!) The teaching chef had told his class, "Cooking is an art, and that art all begins with the little things." Little things...like chopping with the right knife and the right technique!

That initial class and that initial-yet-basic skill of chopping led to many wonderful dishes and meals which Courtney has since been preparing for her family of five and for many fortunate others. Certainly no one in our immediate family will ever forget the nine-course French meal she cooked for our Christmas dinner here in our home one year! Those "little things" had multiplied into splendid gastronomical treats!

Unfortunately, cooking and homemaking are generally seen by our society as necessary evils. In fact, many actually avoid them altogether! The world sees "real life" as being "out there"—in a job, in an office, in a career, in a profession, in a mall, even in a friend's house. Anywhere! Just don't make them stay at home! It seems that we've lost any sense of the importance of the art of homemaking, which includes the art of cooking. We have "the Colonel" down on the corner or "the Clown" at the golden arches to take over our position in the home...and more specifically, in the kitchen!

A Calling (Back!) to Home

Precious sister-in-Christ, *God* in Titus 2:4-5 is sounding forth His high calling to you and me as *His* women "to be homemakers." True, we live *in* the world...but, dear one, we are not *of* the world (John 17:15-16). We are not to live as worldly women live. We are not to be conformed to this world (Romans 12:2). We are not to focus on what worldly women focus on. We are not to seek what worldly women seek. No, as *God's* women and as women who desire to live *godly* lives, we are to focus on being *homemakers*, *home lovers*, and *workers at home*.[1]

Evidently the apostle Paul must have observed the abnegation and/or neglect of the home by the women on the island of Crete, for he instructs "Pastor Titus" to make sure the older women thoroughly "admonish the young women...to be homemakers" (Titus 2:3-5). As we've been learning, these seasoned saints (and homemakers!) were to bring the young women to their senses in this all-important area of their work in the home. Remember, there are only ten essentials for godly living named here in these three verses, and one of them has to do with taking care of the home. Now, in my thinking that makes this calling important! And as I consider that this calling is actually coming from *God,* I can only look to Him for His magnificent and splendid grace...and set about to answer this high calling from Him with my whole heart!

And believe me, when I first stumbled upon this calling in Titus 2:5, a calling to turn my attention homeward, it most definitely required all of God's magnificent and splendid grace for me to do so...and it still does. Growing up in a home with both parents working, I received little training as a girl and young woman in the fine art (or is it the lost art?!) of homemaking. I've had to *learn* how to be a homemaker. Managing and "making" a home is not easily done. And the needed skills are not inherent or natural. It's certainly not second nature or something automatic that comes to us as members of the fairer sex...or comes to us at salvation! No, it's a calling. A dual calling—a calling that the older women are to teach...and a calling that the young women are to learn. (And don't forget, God is honored and exalted and glorified when we heed His callings and when we excel in this essential for godly living as well—verse 5!)

I know I wasn't alone when it came to my ignorance as a new Christian trying to learn how to love my husband and my two little ones...*and* my home. I was clueless! But as I began to grow as a Christian and in my desire to please the Lord in all things, I realized my need in this area of the home, and I sought out others to help me, to teach me, to show me, to guide me. How I thank God (and so does my dear family!) for the understanding women who listened to—and answered—my barrage of questions regarding cleaning products and tools and methods! For the patience of those who actually allowed me to come and watch them clean their house. For the wisdom of those who actually sat down with me and showed me *how* to make a meal menu for the week, a grocery list, and a schedule that would minister to my family as all the "good housekeeping" chores got done! These precious saints and sisters helped me, and I submitted myself to be taught and trained. That's the winning combination outlined in Titus 2:3-5.

A Calling to Care

There's a logic at work in Paul's mind as he points to the older women and the curriculum they are to teach to their younger sisters. The essentials listed in verses 4 and 5 of Titus 2 seem to naturally fall into pairs:

—love of husband and love of children point to personal duty.
—discipline and purity point to personal character.
—homemaking and kindness point to the personal position we maintain in the home.

Some translations of the Bible read "keepers at home" instead of "homemakers," but most scholars agree that "*workers* at home" or "*stayers* at home" or "*busy* at home" is more the meaning.

And there's a reason why Paul wrote these instructions. In 1 Timothy 5:13-14 we learn of a problem some of the women in the church at Ephesus had—they were "idle, wandering about from house to house, and not only idle but also gossips and busybodies, saying things which they ought not" (verse 13). In that same passage, Paul teaches that the solution was for those women (more specifically, the young widows) to "marry, bear children, manage the house, [and] give no opportunity to the adversary to speak reproachfully" (verse 14). In other words, they would then have some *one* to take *care* of and some *place* to take *care* of.

The teaching in Titus 2:3-5 parallels the advice given in 1 Timothy 5:13-14—It is a good thing for women to *be* at home and to be *busy* at home. This instruction carries with it

a condemnation of idleness. And it is for the same purpose—
"that the word of God may not be blasphemed" (Titus 2:5).
Rather than develop a tendency to laziness and looseness
(wandering the freeways and malls), God's *high* calling to us
is a calling *home*—a calling to care for the *place* and for the
people at home. And that calling "calls" for us to *be* at home!

That's the teaching here—*oikourgous* (the Greek word
used for this essential) means working at home. *Oikos* indicates a primary work, a house, a dwelling, the people and
the place; and *ergon* is from a word meaning "to do work,"
used almost 150 times in the Bible to refer to deeds, to work,
and to works. As one gentleman put it, " 'Homeworkers'
describes the *active* housewife, whose *labors* are beyond
measure and whose *efforts* will bless the lives of her children
and husband in countless ways"[2] (emphasis added).

A Calling to Be Queen (...of the Home)

Perhaps my favorite thought on this subject comes from
the commentator who wrote of God's high calling to us to
be *homemakers* as a calling that "sets her position as queen
in the home."[3] I like that. I like that a lot! It puts a regal spin
on our calling—a calling to be "queen in the home." What
new attitudes and insights about homemaking might we
adopt were we to picture ourselves as queens rather than
indentured servants in our home?

1. Homemaking is a *priority*—I love Titus 2:3-5
    because it so clearly spells out God's will for my
    life (and yours, too!) as a Christian woman. I never
    have to wonder what it is God wants me to do
    and be. It's here, in this little passage in the Bible.
    It's black and white (black ink on white paper).
    And one of God's priorities for our life is that we
    be *homemakers*. As one person put it, "the greatest
    priority in a home should be love. If a wife loves

her husband and her children, she is well on the way to making the marriage and the home a success."⁴ And if we view our home as our castle, we'll make it a priority to create an atmosphere of love in the home that is felt by all who dwell there.

2. Homemaking is a *privilege*—Being a queen is a privilege...just as "making" and "building" a home is a privilege. The wise woman sees it as such and sets about the business of building her house, her "castle" if you will (Proverbs 9:1 and 14:1). Indeed, "there is no greater task, responsibility and privilege in this world than to make a home."⁵

3. Homemaking is about *people*—Home is a *place* where *people* live. Without people, a home is merely a house—concrete, board, nails, and shingles. Here in California (and, no doubt, in your state) we have what are called "model homes." When a housing development goes up, the contractors create a little street lined with model homes of the houses that are up for sale. There's no doubt these homes belong in a home-decorating magazine! They are ideal. They are cutting edge. They are showcases of the latest trends and newest colors. Everything is done well...and expensively! Truly, women drool over them and their lovely landscaping, fountains, ponds, and pools. It's all there. (It's not hard to envision yourself as the queen of one of these fine dwellings!)

   But no one lives there. These models are beauty...without a heart. They are houses... without people, without all the life and activity and laughter and interchange that takes place under the roof of a real home.

Who are the people in your home, dear one? Is there a husband to serve? Children to nurture? Aging parents to care for? Or perhaps another woman who's a roommate? If there are people in your life, then you have a home to make!

4. Homemaking is also about a *place*—A model home has no people. That's true. But it's also true that if there are *people* living in your house, then you should make that *place* a lovely home, a place for your loved ones. Maybe there won't be pools and ponds, but there can—and should!—be beauty. There's nothing wrong with taking a page out of the "model-home" book and creating an environment that graces those who reside there. Our sphere and our specialty is to be the home. So why not be the best when it comes to "making" the *place* where we reign, a place of beauty and blessing?

5. Homemaking is a *passion*—not a prison. Being a keeper or stayer or busy at home does not mean that your home is a prison where you must be kept! No, you're the queen! "Caring for the home" is the idea. And because homemaking is God's high calling and an essential for godly living, then why not make it a passion? I have a personal philosophy that I try to live by—if there's anything I must do or have to do, I try to do it with passion. I try to give it my all. I try to be the best at it. Rather than wish it away or begrudge the fact that it must be done, I try to learn how to do it and how to do it well. I own the assignment or the task or the work. I try, with the Lord's help, to accept the challenge and, as the Ultimate Queen of the Home, Proverbs 31 woman did, do

the work "willingly" (Proverbs 31:13). Shouldn't our work be done willingly and passionately? Shouldn't our labors be labors of love? As King Solomon, a wise master home builder, wrote to us queens, "Whatever your hand finds to do, do it with your might" (Ecclesiastes 9:10)!

6. Homemaking is a *profession*—As we all know, homemaking is a challenging and diverse career in itself. Indeed, it is a profession, a noble profession Christian women have embraced down through the centuries. The older women have learned it...mastered it...and taught it to the younger women...who learn it...master it...and then teach it to others...and so the chain of instruction is unbroken. We, too, are to own and master our God-given profession of queen of the home, of managing our household.

And, dear mother, as the mother of two daughters and now two granddaughters, I can't resist adding this heart-thought—we are to teach our daughters first. *They* are the younger women in our lives, the ones God has planted on our doorstep (and in our heart!), the ones God has placed under our very own roof. They are and always will be the priority people in our life. If we never teach homemaking to another woman other than our precious daughters, we have done well. That would mean—with God's grace and blessing—that another precious and priceless generation is on its way to professionalism and to passing on the art of homemaking to another generation. That would mean we have done superbly! We have answered God's high calling to teach good things to younger women.

7. Homemaking is a matter for *prayer*—The simple
    act of praying for our "palace" and our home-
    making and for the loved ones for whom we are
    "making" the home transforms our physical
    efforts into a great spiritual work with eternal
    value. I love this prayer from the heart of an
    unknown person who definitely understood that
    homemaking is a matter for prayer!

My Kitchen Prayer

Lord of all pots and pans and things,
since I've not time to be
A saint by doing lovely things
or watching late with Thee
Or dreaming in the dawn light
or storming Heaven's gates,
Make me a saint by getting meals
and washing up the plates.

Although I must have Martha's hands,
I have a Mary mind,
And when I black the boots and shoes,
Thy sandals, Lord, I find.
I think of how they trod the earth,
each time I scrub the floor;
Accept this meditation Lord,
I haven't time for more.

Warm all the kitchen with Thy love,
and light it with Thy peace;
Forgive me all my worrying
and make my grumbling cease.
Thou who didst love to give men food,
in room or by the sea,
Accept this service that I do,
I do it unto Thee.[6]

8. Homemaking is *permanent*—Our high calling to homemaking is not only an important calling, but it is a permanent calling. Why? Because wherever you are, that's where your home is. In England, the flag is flown atop whichever castle the queen happens to be visiting or residing in. Wherever the queen is, that's the royal home. So, no matter the ages or stages of you or your family, you will always be "making" a home. If you serve on the mission field, your bungalow, clay hut, or bamboo dwelling will be the site for home building and homemaking. If you're living in a two-rom high-rise New York City apartment (like my daughter Katherine and her family) or an apartment in Anytown, USA, your opportunity and privilege is to make that living space a cozy, comfortable, inviting home. If you're on the move (as is my daughter Courtney as a Navy wife), then your temporary housing, the base B.O.Q. (officers temporary quarters), or one room in a military dorm (where Paul and Courtney's family of four lived for three months!!!!!) becomes the setting for homemaking. Even your tent on a family camping outing...or the nursing home where your parents (and you!) finally dwell will call for your homemaking talents and efforts.

9. Homemaking sets a *pattern*—Titus 2:3-5 tells us what the older women are to do—they are to teach "good things" and train and model for others what a godly woman is and what a godly woman does. One of the "things" older women are to teach us is how to be a homemaker.

   Thank God that biblical women have set a pattern for us to follow! Just look at this amazing list of "older women" (and women of old!)—truly, "queens" in their own day—and the pattern they set for you and me (and the "profession" they enjoyed)!

Eve	Occupation: wife, helper, companion, co-manager of Eden
Sarah	Occupation: wife, mother, household manager
Rebekah	Occupation: wife, mother, household manager
Rachel	Occupation: shepherdess, housewife
Hannah	Occupation: homemaker
Mary (Jesus' mother)	Occupation: homemaker[7]

10. Homemaking is a *practice*—and is to be practiced. An excellent (and encouraging!) time-management principle is "repetition is the mother of skill." When we get up every morning with a fresh prayer for our home in our heart and a burning passion for building our home in our soul, when we acknowledge the priority and pledge to better the lives of the people at home by bettering the place of home, and then "practice" the many tasks that such love requires, in time we master the skills of homemaking. And through practice we do them more quickly, even rotely, without effort and without thought, simply because we have practiced and done them so long and so often that they become a part of us...and a home is forged!

And so, dear sister, *any* house, habitation, dwelling, abode, residence, domicile where you and/or your loved ones are called upon by God to live sets the scene for you, the "queen in the home" to do your thing—to make a home!

Looking Upward

Do you ever think about the value of "little things"? Maybe even the *necessity* of "little things"? We began this chapter with the "little things" that contribute to a great meal. And we've considered many of the "little things" that make up our homemaking and that make a house a home.

All of life and its rewards begin with the "little things." The bounty of home begins with the "little things" done out of a large heart of love—love for God and His calling upon your life, and love for your family and home. Let's not underestimate the significance of the "little things" or of "a little place" called home.

A Little Place

"Where shall I work today, dear Lord?"
And my love flowed warm and free.
He answered and said,
"See that little place?
Tend that place for Me."

I answered and said, "Oh no, not there!
No one would ever see.
No matter how well my work was done,
Not that place for me!"

His voice, when He spoke, was soft and kind,
He answered me tenderly,
"Little one, search that heart of thine,
Are you working for them or ME?
Nazareth was a little place...
So was Galilee."[8]

Essential

"...admonish the young women...to be homemakers..."
—TITUS 2:4-5

"Do you ever feel like you were 'born in vain'? Well, take heart! The woman who answers her high callings from God to love husband and children and build a home has 'a high and sacred mission on earth'!"

"She watches over the ways of her household."
—PROVERBS 31:27

"Your home can be a paint-by-number, crude-but-heartless and immature attempt...or a masterpiece worthy to be hung in the halls of heaven, a work of art that truly brings honor and glory to God (not to mention the beauty and joy and order that bring peace of mind and well being to the souls of those who reside there)."

Chapter Eighteen

Homemaking—An Essential for Godly Living

ost women have, at some time in their life, kept a diary. I know I did. In fact, if my parents wanted to give me a "sure" Christmas gift, a diary always did it! And I actually wrote in them! To this day, I am a journaller, delighting in finding each new one and filling it with the nuggets I gather from my study of the Bible, from my pastor's sermons, and from my personal reading. Plus, each journal provides a chronology of the flow of the days of my life... and my husband's... and my children's... and now my grandbabies.

So, of course, I've been greatly blessed by the treasure-of-a-book by Elizabeth Prentiss (1818–1878). It's titled *Stepping Heavenward*, and spans the life of this nineteenth-century Christian woman from age sixteen to her death. In it I've discovered the heart of a woman—a woman who struggled (just like you and I!) with spiritual growth and with answering God's high callings upon her life. In the end, however, we witness her journey of heeding and answering His callings as she sought "More Love to Thee, O Christ" (as the hymn title she wrote so succinctly puts it).

Now, share a glimpse of the treasure in this one entry, expressing the thoughts of a girl with no desire to ever marry. Yet her life was touched by a *home...* and its *homemaker*.

> Aunty has six children of her own, and has adopted two. She [is]... full of fun and energy, flying about the house as on wings, with a kind, bright word for everybody. All her household affairs go on like clockwork; the children are always nicely dressed; nobody ever seems out of humor; nobody is ever sick. Aunty is the central object around which everybody revolves; you can't forget her a moment, for she is always doing something for you, and then her unflagging good humor and cheerfulness keep you good-humored and cheerful. I don't wonder that Uncle Alfred loves her so.
>
> I hope I shall have just such a home. I mean this is the sort of home I would like if I ever married, which I never intend to do. I would like to be just such a bright, loving wife as Aunty is, to have my husband lean on me as Uncle leans on her; to have just as many children, and to train them as wisely and kindly as she does hers. Then, indeed, I would feel that I had not been born in vain, but had a high and sacred mission on earth.[1]

Do you have a home and a family (and a niece!) to love, dear one? Do you have a marriage and family to nurture? Do you have a husband and children to serve? Do you have a home to "make"? And do you ever feel like you were "born in vain"? Well, take it from the heart of Elizabeth Prentiss, who "got it"—the woman who answers her high callings from God to love husband and children and build a home (Proverbs 14:1) has "a high and sacred mission on earth"! When we take our homemaking seriously, it becomes a profession and a pursuit—and a passion—that speaks loudly and blesses many.

What is a home? And what's at the heart of our homemaking? One day I set about to answer this question for myself and arrived at the following insights.

Home Is Where Your Heart Is

We've all heard this warm saying before. But *how* can we turn our heart homeward? Our fast-paced, multi-faceted society does not seem to allow for (or value) nurturing the heart of a homemaker. Well, dear one, these few steps work for me.

1. *Be there.* Um, um, um! This is the big one, the little step we can take that will make the big difference in our home and heart! And isn't that the message in Titus 2:4-5? Many women react to the different wordings of this tiny phrase tucked into God's ten essentials for godly living in Titus 2:3-5. For instance, consider these few translations of the phrase "to be homemakers": "workers at home... homekeepers...good housekeepers...domesticated ...to keep house...keepers at home...stayers at home." I don't know what kind of images come to your mind, but one thing God is clearly asking of us is to just be there! If we'll just be there, then our heart will be there and the work of loving our

home will get done. So... just be there! Take your calendar in hand and set about to prioritize, cancel, schedule, and chart a lifestyle that allows you to simply be at home more often.

2. *Pray.* I know I've mentioned this before, but this bears repeating! Do you realize that the simple act of praying about your homemaking can transform something physical (like dusting, vacuuming, washing, and cooking) into something spiritual? And indeed, homemaking is our spiritual work. After all, as we've been learning, it's one of God's high callings and an essential for godly living. And how much better we do it when we do it heartily, as to the Lord and not to men (Colossians 3:23) and when we do all our homemaking to the glory of God" (1 Corinthians 10:31). And prayer pushes us into such a mind-set! Truly, time on our knees puts energy into our efforts!

3. *Devote 30 minutes a day to some kind of home improvement.* At least begin with half an hour! Sometimes we avoid being at home because it's the scene of chaos and clutter and confusion. Our nooks and crannies and counters and closets are filled with stacks and piles that have become eyesores...and frankly, life is more lovely when we are not having to look at these seemingly-monumental tasks and not having to face such a mess. The scripture from the lips of Jesus applies once more—"where your treasure is, there your heart will be also" (Matthew 6:21). So devote the "treasure" of 30 minutes to bettering your home-sweet-home. That small endeavor will gain dividends in your heart (not to mention in your home!).

4. *Spend time with women who do love and "make" their homes.* Let their love and enthusiasm rub off on you. Sometimes when we are exposed to too much of the world, we lose touch with the vision God has for our home. Godly, older women (younger ones, too!) can refresh the vision and refuel the passion.

5. *Invest in something—a book, a class, a project, a seminar—that sparks your interest in your home.* I know so many women who enjoy scrap-booking—making a picture journal of the lives of their little ones and their loved ones. A project like that will rekindle your heart! Others have invested in classes on quilting (and the fabrics!), flower arranging, cooking (like my Courtney), or home finance. On and on the list goes. Believe me, each investment will increase the heat of your heart for home.

   Speaking of investing, invest in a library of books on homemaking, on speed-cleaning, on time management, on organization, on meal planning, and so on. The younger women I've mentored over the years were asked to read five minutes a day on the home management book of their choice—and, of course, they were welcomed to freely dip into my own "home ec" library.

Home Is the Hub

Who lives in your house? I know *you* do, but who else is blessed (or cursed, whichever shoe fits!) to reside under your roof? As I again read through the portrait of Elizabeth Prentiss's "Aunty" and her home, I saw that her home was the hub of constructive activity and loving family relationships and the many good things in life. I especially love the description of Aunty as "the central object around which everybody revolves." I had the mental image of her on the move, sweeping and swishing through room after room, turning and touching each person in each room, wherever she went—working her magic as she fussed and trifled with the many little things that make up the art of homemaking.

Is that true of you, precious reading sister? Is your home the hub of your life? Does all that is important to you happen at home? Is your heart centered there? Your life? And do you willfully make home the happy hub of life for your beloved family? Imagine the happiness you create when you serve at the center of your home life, doing the work that "makes" your home a happy hub, whirling about your business, managing all things well. May you and I ever be "just such a bright, loving wife" and mother and homemaker as Aunty was!

Home Is a Haven

A haven is a safe place. It's a harbor and a port where vessels and wayfarers find shelter. And shouldn't our homes offer such shelter and safety to our cherished family? Shouldn't our home be a haven of rest for the weary souls that leave its portals each morning and arrive back at dusk? Shouldn't a heart and home of love await each battered and bruised soul who returns to its sanctuary each evening? When night falls (or school is out or work is done), shouldn't there be one place on earth where each person's well-being is important to someone else?

Well, my friend, you and I as homemakers are that *someone else!* And we have the privilege of preserving the health and quality of life of those under our care. I carry in my Bible a tattered copy of a newspaper article from the

Honolulu Advertiser dated Thursday, January 27, 2000, titled "Tiny Kauai snail wins protection—Agency to develop plan for survival." It seems that the creature known as Newcomb's snail—only a quarter-inch in size, a little larger than the head of a nail—is now listed by the U.S. Fish and Wildlife Service as threatened under the Endangered Species Act. As a result, a team of biologists will develop a recovery plan to help the species survive. The outcome is that those who disturb the species in any way are considered to be criminals.

Now, are you wondering *why* I would clip such an article? Why, it's because of the children! Our children, your children, everyone's children! If our government would go to such drastic measures to preserve a tiny brown creature like a *snail* on the remotest island of Hawaii and the farthest western point of the United States, shouldn't we do even more for our children?

Your job, dear mother and homemaker, is to make sure that your children's lives are precious to you, that they are protected, that they have a shelter from the threats to their livelihood. You see, the home is *God's* recovery plan for our family. Perhaps the only way they will survive is if we extend the love and do the work that makes our home a haven. How blessed is the husband and child who can simply come home after the rigors of the day and know that all is well there...and will be well. How blessed they are to have one place—a place you are in charge of—that is a haven, a safe place, a harbor and a shelter for their bodies and souls!

Home Is a Hospital

As I think about this wonderful quality of home, my mind is running in two directions—to two different needs that our precious family members experience and that the hospital called home can take care of.

First, is the area of the physical. Family members need home to be a hospital when they are down with an illness, or when they are recovering from an accident or from surgery. At such times Mom becomes Dr. Mom. At such times outside activities cease while someone (Mom again!) sits by a bed, reads to and aids the suffering one, serves the warm soups and liquids or soothing cool drinks and ice cream that nourish the person and relieve the pain from the ravages of physical trauma, plays the music that ministers to the one who is down...or arranges for the comforting sound of silence.

Second, is the area of the emotional. Jesus said that "in the world you will have tribulation" (John 16:33). And no one in your or my family is immune to this ugly reality! Feelings get hurt. Names are hurled. Poor grades are given out. Relationships are severed. Friends turn away. Abilities are overlooked. Accomplishments go unnoticed and unrewarded. Dreams are dashed. Engagements are ended. Marriages collapse. Jobs disintegrate. Pain comes in a variety package. And *when* it comes (not *if* it comes), you, dear homemaker, once again must "make" your home into a hospital and set about to "nurse" the wounded. We are called upon to mend the hearts that are broken, to nurse the souls that ache, to tend to the downcast, and to strengthen the fainthearted. Home must be the one place our loved ones can count on to hold them up and build them up again.

How blessed is the family member who can rely on your word of comfort when they're weary, your joy in the Lord when they're sad, and your strength in the Lord when they're weak. As Proverbs instruct us, the tongue of the wise promotes health and a merry heart does good, like medicine (Proverbs 12:18 and 17:22).

> *Home is a world of strife shut out,*
> *a world of love shut in.*[2]

Home Is to Be Happy

As you read the descriptions I'm sharing from the Bible and from other sources describing what a home is...and is to be...I'm sure you can see that any home that meets these qualifications is a happy home.

And, you and I, dear home manager and homemaker, have the job assignment of providing the home magic and the homemade medicine of "happiness." Imagine your husband and your child coming home after a hard day to find behind the door at home a waiting and welcoming wife and mother whose life is overflowing with God's joy and a happy heart. May that happy woman be you!

And where does that "happiness" come from? It comes from the Lord—the joy of the Lord is our strength, and the fruit of the Spirit is joy. It comes from the fulfillment we derive from heeding and obeying God's high calling to love our husband, to love our children, and to love our home. Note the "formula" for happiness as presented in the lyrics of the age-old hymn, "Trust and Obey":

> When we walk with the Lord in the light of His
>   Word,
> What a glory He sheds on our way!
> While we do His good will He abides with us still,
> And with all who will trust and *obey*.
> Trust and *obey*, for there's no other way
> To be happy in Jesus, but to trust and *obey*.[3]

Are you walking in the light of God's Word to you as a homemaker? Are you doing His good will as a homemaker? Then happiness is yours and more than likely, your home is a happy one!

Home Is a Hearth

In days gone by (as in the days before electric heaters and central heat!), the hearth at home was the place where family members gathered when coming in from the cold. The family huddled around the hearth, seeking and gaining the warmth of a fire. It was the center of the home. It was, first of all, where food was cooked! The warmth and aroma of "Mom's homemade cooking" greeted each arriver. It was also where the children learned to read and write, where the girls learned to sew. It was where family history was rehearsed. It was where group singing took place. It was where the stories of Jesus were told and prayers were lifted to God.

Now, your home may not contain a hearth. And we're no longer living in the past that these scenes describe. But when I speak of home as being a "hearth," I'm really speaking of a focus—a focus on home and on the family. Of an emotion. Of a feeling that a place called "home" brings to the spirit of man. It's an atmosphere. It's an aura. It's a sensation. It's a warmth. And all of the above should (and can!) be experienced by your family members and extended to all those who cross the enchanting threshold of your *home*. And that home, that hearth that beckons others to its warmth, begins in your own heart of love. As one has well said, "A house is made of walls and beams; a home is built with love and dreams," and "Money can build a house, but it takes love to make it a home."[4]

Home Is for Hospitality

Historically the Christian home has been used to minister not only to family but to strangers who needed a "hotel," a hearth, a haven, a hospital. The word *hospitality* actually indicates "stranger love." And, my friend, it is our privilege to extend such love to outsiders and to join the ranks of the many women of the Bible who used their homes as the scene of ministry:

- The widow of Zarepheth, who welcomed and cared for God's prophet Elijah (1 Kings 17).

- The Shunammite woman, who extended bed and board to God's prophet Elisha (2 Kings 4). .

- Mary, the mother of John Mark, who hosted a church in her home (Acts 12:12-17).

- Lydia, who opened her home to Paul and his missionary team (Acts 16:13-15,40).

- Priscilla and her husband who also hosted a home church (1 Corinthians 16:19).

- The widows who showed hospitality and "lodged strangers" (1 Timothy 5:10).

Looking Upward

Finally, home is you, dear one! And what you are is what your home is. And what you do (or don't do) is what your home becomes. Your home can be a paint-by-number, crude-but-heartless and immature attempt...or a masterpiece worthy to be hung in the halls of heaven, a work of art that truly brings honor and glory to God (not to mention a work of art whose beauty and joy and order bring peace of mind and well-being to the souls of those who reside there). Home is a gift that you choose to give (or not give) to your family.

And making a home is a sacrifice. It's always a sacrifice to get out of bed in the morning, or out of your easy chair in the afternoon, or off your couch in the evening and get the work of home done. But it's our *magnum opus*—our life's crowning work. It's always a sacrifice to do what we *must* do rather than do what we *want* to do. It's always a sacrifice (and a battle!) to get our energies and efforts into gear rather than to lounge and to laze. Your home and homemaking tells the whole watching world, beginning with your precious ones at home, what you are. What you are all about. What your heart is like. And where your heart is. What you value. Whether you're neat or sloppy. Whether you love or loathe your family.

Homemaking is an art, and you (and I!) have the privilege of expressing and developing all your talents there in a little place called home. You get to build...beautify...organize...create...fuss...express yourself. You get to read and study and grow and master nutrition, finances, horticulture, design, wardrobe, etc. And you also get to shape your children, to give their precious lives a bent toward God. To nurture their souls with the good things of God. To pass on the truth about Jesus to one more generation. And to do so means you've got to be dedicated, organized, and a woman of purpose. And you've got to have the spunk and energy to follow through on all the dedication, organization, and purpose that answering God's high calling to homemaking requires.

Oh, that we would embrace this essential for godly living! That we would own and accept God's high calling to homemaking, to make our house a home. That the "journal" of our life would report that *we* have not been born in vain—but that *we* have lived out our high and sacred mission on earth.

10 Essential

"...admonish the young women...to be good..."
—Titus 2:4-5

*"Goodness or kindness means the absence of evil
and selfishness and the presence of a heart set on
bettering the lives of others. Goodness or kindness
is a reflection of the divine character of God."*

Jesus "went about doing good."
—Acts 10:38

*"A watching world cannot keep from seeing the
results of a lifestyle of goodness and kindness,
and the impact is immeasurable as you and
I simply do all the good we can by all the means
we can in all the ways we can in all the
places we can at all the times we can to all the
people we can as long as ever we can."*

Chapter Nineteen

A Woman's High Calling to Goodness

Our family has been most blessed by Jim's mother. You should hear Jim's list of the many "little things" dear Lois did for him! Honestly, she made being his wife hard for me. Why? Because she loved her kitchen and loved filling up Jim and his dad with her homemade delicacies. And she loved to wash, delighting in scrubbing every spot out of every garment that her two "men" would be wearing. And that delight extended itself to her love of ironing—which extended itself to ironing Jim's sheets...and even his underwear! (Now do you see why it was a little hard for me—who was clueless—to come along behind her as Jim's caregiver?!)

But seriously, Jim's mother was a saint! He has a lifetime of vivid and warm memories that center on his childhood home. His mom was always there when he came home from school—even at noon for lunch! And she sat and ate with him, with an ever-ready ear and a kind word of encouragement.

Lois's kindness found its ultimate expression in her own home to those most dear to her. And, as is always true of any vessel that is full, her kindness overflowed to her neighbors, those at her church and in her community—even to many missionaries around the world (as she served as president of her church's Women's Missionary Union). Later, as a widow, Lois gave up her home and moved to the San Fernando Valley just so she could be close to Jim and his family...and minister her lovingkindness to us. And, once again, those at church received the overflow of her goodness, as she drove other widows to church, prepared meals, and encouraged others verbally as well as gave to them monetarily.

Yes, these are "little things," but they are priceless gifts of kindness and goodness offered up by just one little godly girl...who became one little godly wife...who became one little godly mother...who became one little godly mother-in-law...who became one little godly grandmother...who became one little godly widow...who became one little godly saint whose impact was so far-reaching that our church's chapel was filled for her memorial service with those who gave testimony of her many "little" godly deeds.

I pray that this pattern of a godly life spent in godly goodness will be true of me as well. And I pray the same for you, dear one.

Who...Is to Be Good?

Every Christian is called to be *good* and do *good* works (Ephesians 2:10). We see this calling repeated in Titus 3:1 when Paul tells Titus to tell the Christians on the island of Crete "to be ready for every *good* work" (emphasis added).

Every Christian is also called to walk by the Spirit and to show forth God's gracious fruit of the Spirit *goodness* (Galatians 5:16,22-23).

In our quest to understand God's high calling to us as women, we are most interested in God's dual calling to goodness. *First*, the older women are to be teachers of "*good things*" (Titus 2:3). And what did the teaching curriculum include? That they teach the young women to be *good* (verse 5). (And, as we've repeatedly noted, for the older women to be able to teach the young women this essential for godly living, it is understood that those older women had previously learned the trait of *goodness* themselves!) And *second*, the young women are to submit themselves to be taught how to be good.

And don't forget the context of our three verses from Titus 2—these younger women are wives and mothers and home managers. And God is calling them to be *good* (as in *kind*) wives, mothers, and home managers! In other words, they are not to rule their households with an iron hand, but practice the law of kindness and goodness.[1] (I do repeat, however—*all* women, married or single or widowed, old or young, are called to be kind and good!)

The classic example of a woman in the Bible who was good and kind is Dorcas. It was said of her that she was "full of good works and charitable deeds" (Acts 9:36). This dear, kind woman had made such an impact with her good deeds that at her death, the local Christians sent for the apostle Peter, hoping he could do something about their loss. When Peter arrived at their place in Lydda where Dorcas's body was laid, he was met by a multitude of widows who showed him many of the robes Dorcas had made for them. (Remember, everything was made by hand, so it's quite possible each robe took several months to make!) The life of Dorcas backs up this thought—"The value of our good is not measured by what it costs us, but by the amount of good it does the one concerned."[2]

Can you begin to envision the impact you and I can have as women who do good for others? That was what Paul wanted the older women to communicate to the younger women—that, by being good and kind, the church and its people would be blessed and the younger women would be a blessing, first to their own families and also to the church body.

What...Does It Mean to Be Good?

"Good" is the English translation of the Greek word *agathas*. And scholars go back and forth between translating *agathas* as "good" and "kind." For our purposes, I'll use the two words together so we can enjoy the full flavor of the meaning of this all-important term.

So then, what does it mean to be good and kind? It means to be gentle, to be considerate and sympathetic, to be amiable and congenial.[3] Therefore, as the mistress of the house, wives, mothers, and homemakers are to add to their thrift, energy, and personal discipline the mark of a good and kind manner—a benign, gracious, heartily kind demeanor.[4]

You know by now that the Proverbs 31 Woman is a favorite lifetime study of mine. And of her it is said, "She does [her husband] good and not evil all the days of her life," and "She opens her mouth with wisdom, and on her tongue is the law of kindness" (Proverbs 31:12 and 26). This beautiful-on-the-inside wife was intent on lavishing every possible good upon her husband. She lived to love him, and so she did him good at every opportunity. In fact, she willfully set about to operate her life and his home in a way that routinely benefited him with good.[5] And when it came to her speech, she set an example for us as well, an example of setting "a law" to guide her choice of words, "the law of kindness." In other words, if what she was about to say wasn't wise and wasn't kind, those words were never uttered.

And one more thing about goodness and kindness—it is often contrasted with evil. For instance, as in the verse above, this "good" wife did her husband *good* and not *evil*. In the case of the righteous man Job, he is described as a *good* man who feared God and stayed away from *evil* (Job 1:1). Joseph, in the Old Testament, when he spoke to his brothers about their sinful behavior toward him, said, "You meant *evil* against me; but God meant it for *good*..." (Genesis 50:20, emphasis added).

All summed up, we could say—Goodness or kindness means the *absence* of evil and selfishness and the *presence* of a heart set on bettering the lives of others. Goodness or kindness is a reflection of the divine character of God, for, as my pastor writes, "to be kind is to be godlike."[6]

Where...Is Goodness to Occur?

Obviously all of life is a stage for our goodness and kindness. And obviously every person who crosses our path is a candidate for receiving our goodness and kindness. As someone has noted, "Wherever there is a human being there is an opportunity for kindness."

But our passage in Titus 2 is mainly focused on the home...and on our roles as wives, mothers, and homemakers. Therefore, as one scholar writes, "In her position as queen in the home she will be gentle and considerate as she dispenses all that is good and beneficial in this domain."[7]

I know we studied in our previous two chapters about the "little things" that we as "the queen" in our home can do for our dear loved ones. But here's another thought about some more "little things" we can do right in our own home.

Kindness is love doing little things, things that seem scarcely worth doing, and yet which mean much to those for whom they are wrought. Kindness lends a hand when another is burdened. It speaks the cheerful word when a heart is discouraged. It gives a cup of cold water when one is thirsty. It is always doing good turns to somebody. It goes about performing little ministries with a touch of blessing. It scatters its favors everywhere. Few qualities do more to make a life bright and beautiful! Lord, make me kind today...![8]

When...Are We to Be Good?

I love sharing this favorite saying by the famous (and godly and good!) John Wesley. This man made goodness one of his rules to live by. He wrote:

> Do all the good you can,
> by all the means you can,
> in all the ways you can,
> in all the places you can,
> at all the times you can,
> to all the people you can,
> as long as ever you can.

That about says it all, doesn't it? God calls you and me to be good and kind in our home and to our husband and to our children...no matter what kind of home we have or what kind of husband or children live there.

In the days of this teaching from Paul to Titus, the world had little or no Christian influence. Instead, the world was dominated by pagan religions. These religions were immoral and cruel in their practices. And the governments of the day were also cruel and barbaric. Doing good was a foreign concept to that day and age. So any act of kindness was countercultural. You can imagine the impact Christianity began to have as little bands of Christians—like the ones on the island of Crete where Titus pastored—began to perform a multitude of "little" deeds of kindness in everyday life.

Does the culture of that day remind you of the world today? Of the world in which we live? Pick up any newspaper. Turn on any TV news program. What do you see? You see a cruel world and cruel people doing cruel acts. You and I as godly women can influence such a world. How? Not by going out into the world. And not by joining active causes. And not by marching and picketing. But by beginning right in our home. By being kind and good to our family, our husband and children. By speaking a word of kindness to our neighbor and by touching lives in as many "little" ways as we can. By serving one another in the church with deeds of kindness and goodness. A watching world cannot keep from seeing the results of a lifestyle of goodness and kindness, and the impact will be immeasurable as you and I simply do all the good we can by all the means we can in all the ways we can in all the places we can at all the times we can to all the people we can as long as ever we can.

Why...Are We to Be Good?

I can think of five reasons right away why you and I are to be kind and good. We are to be kind and good...

1. *Because kindness and goodness is commanded.*
    The ten essentials listed in Titus 2:3-5 are not
    optional for us as women—they are commanded!
    Paul is commanding Titus...who is to command
    the older women...who are to command the
    younger women...to be kind and good. Such a

dual trait is the nature and essence of God and godliness. As Paul wrote elsewhere, "Therefore, as we have opportunity, let us do good to all..." (Galatians 6:10).

2. *Because kindness and goodness is what a godly woman is all about.* Kindness or goodness is one of the essentials for godly living listed in Titus 2:3-5. The godly widow described in 1 Timothy 5:10 was one who was "well reported for good works." And what were a few of those deeds of kindness, those good works? She "brought up children, lodged strangers, washed the saints' feet, relieved the afflicted, and diligently followed every good work."

3. *Because kindness and goodness blesses our husband and children.* The *people* at home are to receive the first fruits of our kindness and goodness. As someone has quipped, "Home is the place where our stomachs get three square meals a day and our hearts a thousand!" A meal may seem like a little thing, but to our loved ones it's a large one! I like the "large" hint one gentleman provided for us as wives when he said, "The kitchen provides an eloquent pulpit for the application of the biblical call to love your husband." And don't limit your kindnesses to the kitchen. Every minute of every day is an opportunity for expressing this godly essential of goodness...and in every room of your house...and to every member of your household.

4. *Because kindness and goodness blesses our home.* The *place* of home, too, is blessed when we put on not only our work apron, but also a heart of

kindness (Colossians 3:12). Happy the home where kindness dwells!

> A house is built of logs and stones, of tiles
>   and posts and tiers;
> A home is built of loving deeds that stand
>   a thousand years.[9]

5. *Because kindness and goodness brings honor to God.* We've talked at length about the many "little things" that you and I can do that are kind and good. But there is one "big thing" that such acts accomplish—*God* is honored and *God* is glorified. The great purpose clause of Titus 2:5 explains the ultimate *why* for our obedience to all ten of these essentials for godly living—"that the word of God may not be blasphemed." It's frightening and sobering to realize that our conduct is "an advertisement"—good or bad, for or against—the gospel of Jesus Christ. One Bible commentator explains the purpose clause in verse 5 and tells us the one main, large reason why you and I, whether we're in the older- or younger-woman category, are "to be good":

> Wrong conduct on the part of the young married women would easily lead to slanderous remarks with respect to the gospel. Not only [did] the Greeks judge a doctrine by its practical effect upon everyday life but so does the world in general. If young mothers, professing to be Christians, should manifest lack of love for their husbands and for their children, lack of self-control, of purity, domesticity, kindness, and submissiveness, they would cause the message

of salvation to be evil spoken of by outsiders. It must be borne in mind moreover,
that when Paul says "in order that the
word of God may not be reviled," he
means, "in order that the word of God
may be honored."[10]

Now *that's* a high calling!

Looking Upward

And now I want us to look upward, to *really* look
upward! I want us to look at Jesus. As the apostle Peter
sought to find the words that would describe our precious
Jesus to a group of unbelievers, he finally characterized our
Savior as God's anointed One who "went about doing good"
(Acts 10:38). Jesus, again and as always and in everything,
is our example of what should distinguish our lives as
women professing godliness. Being good and doing good
should permeate our lives. As Peter went on to say, Jesus
"went about doing good...healing all who were oppressed."
What a wonderful opportunity we have as women, wives,
mothers, daughters, daughters-in-law and sisters-in-law,
neighbors, and fellow-church members to spend our lives
doing good and offering a kind, healing hand to all who are
oppressed! As Saint Francis of Assisi prayed,

> Lord, grant that I may seek rather
> to comfort—than to be comforted;
> to understand—than to be understood;
> to love—than to be loved.

Essential 10

"...admonish the young women...to be good..."
—TITUS 2:4-5

"I shall pass through this world but once. Any good therefore that I can do or any kindness that I can show to any human being, let me do it now. Let me not defer or neglect it, for I shall not pass this way again."
—AUTHOR UNKNOWN

"There are 'things' we can—and must—do to nurture the basics of godliness. But Christian character is not expressed by good doing. It is to be God-like, to be like God. Doing the right thing is never enough. No, we must have God's image stamped upon our souls. Our hearts must belong to Him and beat along with His. Our desires must be His desires. And our every deed must be marked by His presence. Ours must be a soul that is stamped by the image and superscription of God."

Chapter Twenty

Goodness—An Essential for Godly Living

ave you heard "the tale of two sisters"? Their names are Mary and Martha. These two sisters lived in the day of Jesus. And they had a house in Bethany. They used their home for hospitality, especially toward Jesus and His twelve disciples. In fact, we can read about two of the times they opened their hearts and their home to the Master and His men (Luke 10:38-42 and John 12:2-3).

But I'm thinking of the first such scene. Let's join these two female siblings and see exactly what happened when Jesus came to their house—and learn a few lessons in the practicalities of goodness and kindness.

> Now it happened as they went that He entered a certain village; and a certain woman named Martha welcomed Him into her house. And she had a sister called Mary, who also sat at Jesus'

> feet and heard His word. But Martha was distracted with much serving, and she approached Him and said, "Lord, do You not care that my sister has left me to serve alone? Therefore tell her to help me." And Jesus answered and said to her, "Martha, Martha, you are worried and troubled about many things. But one thing is needed, and Mary has chosen that good part, which will not be taken away from her" (Luke 10:38-42).

In these few verses, we learn a few "things" about how—and how not to—"make" a home! Life is filled with pressure from many sources...and the same was true for Mary and Martha. Yet each handled the pressure of Jesus' visit to their home differently. Both warmly welcomed the Lord and His co-laborers. And both helped with the meal preparations. And both helped with the serving.

But at a certain point each woman began to handle their encounter with Jesus differently. Martha became preoccupied with her work...which led to anxiety...which led to irritation...which led to an outburst of anger and frustration.

Mary, on the other hand, rested at the Lord's feet while Martha was restless. She worshiped while Martha worried. She was at peace while Martha's panic level rose, and rose, and rose! She was sitting while Martha was stewing. And she was listening while Martha was lashing out.

Unfortunately, the gallant and hospitable homemaker Martha serves us as a negative illustration of a good thing gone awry. Martha did the deeds of goodness, but in this instance, she did them without a heart of kindness and goodness. She crossed the line of doing a good thing into doing the works of the flesh. We witness her complaining, blaming, slandering, accusing, and being out of control. Martha-the-meal-manager became Martha-the-mouth. Why? She was looking at her workload and not at the Lord. She was working without worshiping. She was doing her tasks herself instead of unto the Lord. In the end, dinner at Martha's home became a good thing gone sour. Her service in this instance was characterized by carnality.

As I said, we learn a few "things" from these two sisters about how—and how not to—"make" a home! And that's the message Paul is driving home to Titus and the message he wants the older women to drive home to the younger ones—that it's one thing to be a homemaker and to master the skills of this high calling. It's one thing to be organized and to excel at all our good-housekeeping chores. But, when we slip away from doing our duties out of a heart of kindness and goodness, we have slipped in our quest for godly living. We've all seen others (and done it ourselves!) who do all the right "things" when it comes to managing a home. But in their drive toward accomplishing a task or a goal, they overlook "the weightier 'things' of the law" (as Jesus called them)—things like mercy...and I would add, goodness and kindness.

In the preceding chapter we considered the *who*, *what*, *where*, *when*, and *why* of goodness and kindness. And now, in this chapter, I want us to consider the *how*.

How...Are We to Be Good?

As I tried to imagine meeting across my breakfast table with a younger woman (and remembered the many such meetings that have occurred in my kitchen during the past 25 years), and as I tried to imagine such a young woman asking me, "Yes, but *how* can I grow in this goodness God calls me to?", I also tried to imagine what I would tell her from the Word of God. Here's my list (and feel free to add your own advice to it!).

1. *Prepare your heart for goodness*—Nothing so prepares the way for a day of goodness and kindness

as time spent in God's Word. The psalmist describes the Holy Scriptures as perfect, sure, right, pure, clean, true and righteous altogether (Psalm 19:7-9).

What will be the blessed effects of reading your Bible? And what will you find between the thin covers of this great and mighty book? You will find your soul awakened to all that is good and holy. You will come face to face with your many sacred, God-assigned duties. You will find the things of this world growing strangely dim as you turn your heart and mind toward heaven. You will fine tune all the powers of your soul to worship and adoration. You will find a path cleared for your prayers. You will find your soul purified of its many poor and silly passions by the pure Word of the Lord. And you will find your heart carried nearer to heaven.

Surely many noble deeds of kindness and goodness would break forth from such preparation of the heart!

2. *Pray for kindness and goodness*—I have a marvelous, out-of-print book on prayer that "prompts" prayer in different areas of life each day. I've mentioned this before, but here's the prompt that has most changed my life in this great area of goodness. Truly, it has assisted me in answering God's high calling in this essential area of godliness! It simply reads, "Pray for greater love and compassion for others." I can certainly witness to the fact that following through on the prompt and lifting up prayers to God for His love and compassion toward others has changed my heart. Even my husband has noticed a marked difference in me in this area over the years. (Praise

God!) It's as if I now look at others through eyes of love.

And while you're praying, consider this unknown person's prayer and perspective on our deeds of kindness!

> *A Prayer for Kindness and Goodness*
>
> I shall pass through this world but once. Any good therefore that I can do or any kindness that I can show to any human being, let me do it now. Let me not defer or neglect it, for I shall not pass this way again.

3. *Plan for kindness*—I know I shared with you about my wonderful weekly planner that has been the catalyst to new energy in following through on the many disciplines I desire in my life. One category I create each week is for my family and another is for my friends. Under these categories I list names and then at least one act of kindness I would like to extend to each person during the week. Then I transfer these acts to my daily plan. What a joy it's been to plan for kindness. We're all busy, but may the Lord help us to never be too busy for kindness and goodness! The woman who is good dispenses what is good and beneficial. Just as a pharmacist dispenses the medicines that will heal, so we plan to dispense the medicines that promote the lives of others.

And don't forget to act on your plan! Be as kind as you can *today*. You cannot do a kindness too soon, because you never know how soon it will be too late!

4. *Pore over the life of Christ*—Some years (more like decades!) ago, my Jim suggested that we as a couple read through the life of Christ every three months, or four times a year. I was shocked at first! It sounded impossible...on top of an already seemingly impossible schedule built around a busy and bustling household and a man in the ministry. But then Jim explained—all it would take was reading one chapter a day, about five minutes at the most! You see, it was another one of those "little things." Well, over time that little thing has added up to a lot! I'm sure you can imagine the blessings that would arrive each day as you touched and tasted and handled just one chapter of our Savior's exemplary life!

    And, as we've already noticed, His was a life of goodness...as He went about doing good (Acts 10:38). I invite you also to pore over the life of Christ—just one chapter a day, just five minutes a day. When you do you'll witness how...

    > Jesus stopped to touch and heal the leper.
    > Jesus stopped to raise the widow's son.
    > Jesus stopped to heal the woman with the
    > issue of blood.
    > Jesus stopped to touch and heal the
    > woman's bent-over back.
    > Jesus held and blessed the little children.
    > Jesus stopped to heal the blind man beside
    > the road.
    > Jesus stopped to talk to Zacchaeus.

    As you can see, these are just a few of the wonderful acts of Jesus' kindness...all found in the book of Luke, just one of the four wonderful Gospels. Now, *you* do your own study. Pore over the life of your Savior each and every day, keep a running record of His goodness and kindness, and "go and do likewise" (Luke 10:37)!

5. *Peruse the women of the Bible*—I've already mentioned many of these good women who were known for their many good works and kind acts—the Shunammite woman, the widow of Zarephath, Mary and Martha, Dorcas, Lydia. But as the prolific writer of the book of Hebrews finally said when trying to enumerate the many men and women of the Bible who exhibited great faith, "And what more shall I say? For the time would fail me to tell of..." all the rest (Hebrews 11:32). That's how I'm feeling right now. There just isn't time left or space available to share the multitude of good deeds of kindness done by God's women of the Bible. So I'll leave you with the assignment to peruse the women of the Bible on your own. Believe me, you're in for a treat!

6. *Put away all that is not kind and good*—We've already learned that a godly woman is a good and kind woman—she is free from all that is envious, jealous, stingy, and petty. There is nothing evil, cruel, or irritable in her manner. No, she has answered another of God's callings, a calling to put away, to put aside, to strip off, and to rid herself of all unkind deeds and behaviors (Colossians 3:5-9). She has looked to the Lord for His help in putting off "anger, wrath, malice, blasphemy, filthy language" (verse 8).

   May we never be guilty of dishing out poison like the woman in Proverbs 19 whose contentious ways and nagging words were like the continual and persistent dripping of water (verse 13)! Or like the woman in Proverbs 21 who was a cantankerous and "brawling woman" (verse 9, KJV).

Do you need to make a list, dear one? Perhaps a prayer list? Are your deeds those that "drip" with kindness? That edify and minister to your loved ones? That honor the Lord? Or are there a few that need to be stripped off? The picture here is of dirty clothes being stripped off and put aside because they are too soiled to wear.

7. *Put on a heart of kindness*—As we noted in the previous chapter, to be kind and good means to be considerate, amiable, congenial, sympathetic—to be godlike. A kind and good woman is benign, gracious, and possesses a heartily kind demeanor. We are told—indeed, commanded!— to "put on tender mercies [and] kindness" (Colossians 3:12). After we've dealt with those attitudes and behaviors that must be removed from the life of any woman who seeks godliness, we are then to put on the better wardrobe of Christlike kindness and goodness. And that's what this chapter has been all about—about preparing your heart for goodness, about praying for kindness and goodness, about planning for kindness, about poring over the life of Christ, about perusing the women of the Bible, and about putting away all that is not good. Now, just as you go to your closet each fresh new day and carefully select what you will wear, go to God's closet and choose a Spirit-filled wardrobe...and put on a heart of kindness.

Looking Upward

In this chapter we've been considering the *how* of goodness and of godly living. And I hope and pray that the seven "steps" we looked at have been helpful. However, there is one final "step" for you and me, my faithful reading friend. And this step is required, not only for kindness and goodness, but for all ten of the essentials for godly living that we've been attempting to master throughout this book. For us to answer God's high callings, we must look to Him. We must walk with Him. We must rely on Him. We must submit to Him. This is what it means to "walk in the Spirit" (Galatians 5:16).

Yes, there are "things" we can—and must—do to nurture these basics of godliness. We've looked at many and named a number. But Christian character is not expressed by good doing. It is, as noted earlier, to be godlike, to be like God. We must—and should—seek godliness, godly speech, personal discipline, and a ministry of encouraging others. And we must—and should—seek to love our husbands and children, to walk in wisdom and purity, to excel at our homemaking, and in doing good.

But, my friend, you and I both know that in God's economy, such seeking and doing is not enough for us to become the godly women He is calling us to be and our hearts are desiring to be. Doing the right thing is never enough. No, we must have *God's* image stamped upon our souls. Our hearts must belong to *Him* and beat along with *His*. Our desires must be *His* desires. And our every deed must be marked by *His* presence. Ours must be a soul that is stamped by the image and superscription of *God*.

And so, precious one, we must look to God for His grace and for His power to perfect these godly qualities in our lives. And when we do look to Him, those nearest and dearest to us will be blessed and all will see our "light" (His light) shining forth and see our good works (His good works) and will glorify...not us, but...our Father in heaven (Matthew 5:16).

Now, let's pray "A Prayer for Godly Living" along with the women at the beginning of our book. Let's pray along with their hearts and heartfelt words, "Lord, help me to be a godly woman!"

Bibliography

Barclay, William. *The Letters to Timothy, Titus, and Philemon,* revised edition. Philadelphia: Westminster Press, 1975.

Barton, Bruce B. and David R. Veerman and Neil Wilson. *Life Application Bible Commentary—1 Timothy, 2 Timothy, Titus.* Wheaton, IL: Tyndale House Publishers, Inc., 1993.

Getz, Gene A. *The Measure of a Woman.* Glendale, CA: Regal-G/L Publications, 1977.

Guthrie, Donald. *New Testament Commentaries—The Pastoral Epistles.* Grand Rapids, MI: Wm. B. Eerdmans Publishing Company, 1976.

Hendricksen, William. *New Testament Commentary—The Pastoral Epistles.* Grand Rapids, MI: Baker Book House, 1976.

Hiebert, D. Edmond. *Everyman's Bible Commentary—Titus and Philemon.* Chicago: Moody Press, 1957.

Kent, Homer A. Jr. *The Pastoral Epistles.* Chicago: Moody Press, 1977.

MacArthur, John. *The MacArthur Study Bible.* Nashville: Word Publishing, 1997.

MacArthur, John Jr. *The MacArthur New Testament Commentary—Titus.* Chicago: Moody Press, 1996.

Vincent, Marvin R. *Word Studies in the New Testament.* Grand Rapids, MI: Wm. B. Eerdmans Publishing Company, 1973.

Vine, W. E. *An Expository Dictionary of New Testament Words—Volume 4.* Old Tappan, NJ: Fleming H. Revell Company, 1966.

Wiersbe, Warren W. *Be Faithful.* Colorado Springs: Chariot Victor Publishing, 1981.

otes

Chapter 1—A Woman's High Calling to Godliness

1. Donald Guthrie, *Tyndale New Testament Commentaries—The Pastoral Epistles*, quoting Dibelius and Lock (Grand Rapids: Wm. B. Eerdmans Publishing Company, 1976), p. 192.

2. D. Edmond Hiebert, *Everyman's Bible Commentary—Titus and Philemon* (Chicago: Moody Press, 1957), p. 49.

3. Ibid.

4. John MacArthur, Jr., *The MacArthur New Testament Commentary—Titus* (Chicago: Moody Press, 1996), p. 77.

5. Ibid.

6. Albert M. Wells, Jr., *Inspiring Quotations—Contemporary & Classical*, quoting J. H. Morrison (Nashville: Thomas Nelson Publishers, 1988), p. 221.

7. Irving L. Jensen, *Enjoy Your Bible*, quoting William Law in the classic work, *A Serious Call to the Devout and Holy Life* (Minneapolis: World Wide Publications, 1969).

8. William Hendricksen, *New Testament Commentary—Exposition of the Pastoral Epistles*, quoting Horatius Bonar, 1866 (Grand Rapids: Baker Book House, 1976), p. 364.

9. Eleanor L. Doan, ed., *The Speaker's Sourcebook*, source unknown (Grand Rapids: Zondervan Publishing House, 1977), p. 28.

Chapter 2—Godliness—An Essential for Godly Living

1. H. D. M. Spence and Joseph S. Exell, eds., *The Pulpit Commentary, Volume 21* (Grand Rapids: Wm. B. Eerdmans Publishing Company, 1978), p. 24.

2. Hymn by Helen H. Lemmel.

3. Lorne Sanny, *Memorize the Word* (Moody Correspondence School, 820 North LaSalle Street, Chicago IL 60610, 1-800-621-7105), 1980.

4. Hymn by Johann J. Schütz.

5. Benjamin R. DeJong, *Uncle Ben's Quotebook* (Grand Rapids: Baker Book House, 1977), p. 80.

6. Ibid., p. 81.

7. Albert M. Wells, Jr., *Inspiring Quotations—Contemporary & Classical*, quoting Augustine, p. 29.

Chapter 3—A Woman's High Calling to Godly Speech

1. Curtis Vaughan, ed., *The New Testament from 26 Translations* (Grand Rapids: Zondervan Publishing House, 1967), p. 1017.

2. Gene A. Getz, *The Measure of a Woman* (Glendale, CA: Regal–Gospel Light Publications, 1977), pp. 28-29.

3. Elizabeth George, *A Woman After God's Own Heart* (Eugene, OR: Harvest House Publishers, 1997), pp. 38-39.

Chapter 4—Godly Speech—An Essential for Godly Living

1. A. Naismith, *1200 Notes, Quotes, and Anecdotes* (London: Pickering & Inglis Ltd., 1975), p. 186.

2. William Barclay, *The Letters to Timothy, Titus, and Philemon*, rev. ed. (Philadelphia: The Westminster Press, 1975), p. 86.

3. Charles R. Swindoll, *David: A Man of Passion & Destiny* (Dallas: Word Publishing, Inc., 1997), p. 93.

4. M. R. DeHaan and H. G. Bosch, *Bread for Each Day* (Grand Rapids: Zondervan Publishing House, 1980), December 27.

5. A. Naismith, *A Treasury of Notes, Quotes, and Anecdotes* (Grand Rapids: Baker Book House, 1976), p. 97.

Chapter 5—A Woman's High Calling to Personal Discipline

1. J. Oswald Sanders, *Spiritual Leadership*, revised edition (Chicago: Moody Press, 1980), pp. 71-72.

2. Curtis Vaughan, *The New Testament from 26 Translations,* citing The Twentieth Century New Testament (Grand Rapids: Zondervan Publishing House, 1967), p. 1017.

3. Charles Caldwell Ryrie, *The Ryrie Study Bible* (Chicago: Moody Press, 1976), p. 1832.

4. Curtis Vaughan, *The New Testament from 26 Translations,* citing The New English Bible, The New Testament in Basic English, and The New Testament in Modern English respectively, p. 1017.

5. Marvin R. Vincent, *Word Studies in the New Testament*—Vol. I (Grand Rapids: Wm. B. Eerdmans Publishing Co., 1973), p. 636.

6. Drawn from *The Zondervan Pictorial Encyclopedia of the Bible*—Volumes One and Two, Merrill C. Tenney, gen. ed. (Grand Rapids: Zondervan Publishing House, 1975).

7. D. Edmond Hiebert, *Everyman's Bible Commentary—Titus and Philemon* (Chicago: Moody Press, 1957), p. 49.

8. William Hendriksen, *New Testament Commentary—The Pastoral Epistles*, (Grand Rapids: Baker Book House, 1976), p. 312.

Chapter 6—Personal Discipline—An Essential for Godly Living

1. J. D. Douglas, ed., *The New Bible Dictionary* (Grand Rapids: Wm. B. Eerdmans Publishing Co., 1978), p. 1242.

2. John MacArthur, Jr., *The MacArthur New Testament Commentary—Romans 9-16* (Chicago: Moody Press, 1994), p. 269.

3. From the hymn "Turn Your Eyes upon Jesus" by Helen H. Lemmel.

4. Elizabeth George, *A Woman's High Calling Growth and Study Guide* (Eugene, OR: Harvest House Publishers, 2001).

Chapter 7—A Woman's High Calling to Encourage Others

1. Curtis Vaughan, *The New Testament from 26 Translations*, (Grand Rapids: Zondervan Publishing House, 1967), p. 1017.

2. John MacArthur, Jr., *The MacArthur New Testament Commentary—Titus* (Chicago: Moody Press, 1996), p. 78.

3. D. Edmond Hiebert, *Everyman's Bible Commentary—Titus and Philemon* (Chicago: Moody Press, 1957), p. 50.

4. Warren W. Wiersbe, *Be Faithful* (Colorado Springs: Chariot Victor Publishing, 1981), p. 105.

5. John MacArthur, Jr., *The MacArthur New Testament Commentary—Titus*, p. 78.

6. Ibid., p. 78-79.

7. William Barclay, *The Letters to Timothy, Titus, and Philemon*, revised edition (Philadelphia: Westminster Press, 1975), pp. 248-49.

Chapter 8—Encouraging Others—An Essential for Godly Living

1. Homer Kent, *The Pastoral Epistles—Studies in I and II Timothy* (Chicago: Moody Press, 1958), p. 50.

Chapter 9—A Woman's High Calling to Her Marraige

1. W. E. Vine, *An Expository Dictionary of New Testament Words*— Volume 4 (Old Tappan, NJ: Fleming H. Revell Company, 1966), p. 86.

2. Gene A. Getz, *The Measure of a Woman*, (Glendale, CA: Regal–Gospel Light Publications, 1977), p. 73.

3 John MacArthur, Jr., *The MacArthur New Testament Commentary—Titus* (Chicago: Moody Press, 1996), p. 83.

4. Getz, *The Measure of a Woman*, p. 75.

5. Elizabeth George, *A Woman After God's Own Heart* (Eugene, OR: Harvest House Publishers, 1997).

6. Bruce B. Barton, David R. Veerman, and Neil Wilson, *Life Application Bible Commentary—1 Timothy, 2 Timothy, Titus* (Wheaton, IL: Tyndale House Publishers, Inc., 1993), p. 269.

Chapter 10—Loving Your Husband—An Essential for Godly Living

1. Warren W. Wiersbe, *Be Faithful* (Colorado Springs: Chariot Victor Publishing, 1981), p. 105.

2. Curtis Vaughan, ed., *The New Testament from 26 Translations* (Grand Rapids: Zondervan Publishing House, 1967), p.1017.

3. John MacArthur, Jr., *The MacArthur New Testament Commentary—Titus* (Chicago: Moody Press, 1996), p. 83.

4. D. Edmond Hiebert, *Everyman's Bible Commentary—Titus and Philemon* (Chicago: Moody Press, 1957), p. 50.

5. William Barclay, *The Letters to the Galatians and Ephesians*, rev. ed. (Philadelphia: The Westminster Press, 1976), p. 50.

6. MacArthur, Jr., *Titus,* p. 84.

7. Gene A. Getz, *The Measure of a Woman* (Glendale, CA: Regal–Gospel Light Publications, 1977), p. 77.

8. MacArthur, Jr., *Titus,* p. 84.

9. Frank Outlaw.

10. Connie Alexander Huddleston, *Partnership* magazine, January-February, 1986, p. 26.

Chapter 11—A Woman's High Calling to Her Family

1. D. Edmond Hiebert, *Everyman's Bible Commentary—Titus and Philemon*, quoting H. Harvey (Chicago: Moody Press, 1957), p. 50.

2. Homer A. Kent, Jr., *The Pastoral Epistles* (Chicago: Moody Press, 1977), p. 229.

3. Donald Guthrie, *New Testament Commentaries—The Pastoral Epistles* (Grand Rapids: Wm. B. Eerdmans Publishing Company, 1976), p. 193.

4. John MacArthur, Jr., *The MacArthur New Testament Commentary—Titus* (Chicago: Moody Press, 1996), p. 85.

5. Marvin R. Vincent, *Word Studies in the New Testament* (Grand Rapids: Wm. B. Eerdmans Publishing Company, 1973), p. 341.

6. John MacArthur, *The MacArthur Study Bible* (Nashville: Word Publishing, 1997), p. 1864.

7. Albert M. Wells, Jr., *Inspiring Quotations—Contemporary & Classical* (Nashville: Thomas Nelson Publishers, 1988), p. 136.

8. Fred H. Wight, *Manners and Customs of Bible Lands* (Chicago: Moody Press, 1978), pp. 109-22.

9. Frank S. Mead, *12,000 Religious Quotations* (Grand Rapids: Baker Book House, 1989), p. 313.

Chapter 12—Loving Your Family—An Essential for Godly Living

1. Dennis and Dawn Wilson, *Christian Parenting in the Information Age—Rediscovering a Biblical Worldview for Raising Children*, quoting Richard Baxter, *A Christian Directory* (West Jordan, Utah: TriCord Publishing, 1996), p. 186.

2. Frank S. Mead, *12,000 Religious Quotations*, quoting Abbé Felicité Robert de Lamennais (Grand Rapids, Baker Book House, 1989) p. 313.

3. D. L. Moody, *Thoughts from My Library* (Grand Rapids: Baker Book House, 1979), p. 122.

4. John MacArthur, Jr., *The MacArthur New Testament Commentary—Titus*, (Chicago: Moodly Press, 1996), p. 85.

5. Tedd Tripp, *Shepherding a Child's Heart* (Wapwallopen, PA: Shepherd Press, 1995), p. 39.

Chapter 13—A Woman's High Calling to Wisdom

1. Donald Guthrie, *New Testament Commentaries—The Pastoral Epistles* (Grand Rapids: Wm. B. Eerdmans Publishing Company, 1976), p. 193.

2. D. Edmond Hiebert, *Everyman's Bible Commentary—Titus and Philemon* (Chicago: Moody Press, 1957), p. 50.

3. William Barclay, *The Letters of James and Peter*, rev. ed. (Philadelphia: The Westminster Press, 1976), p. 249.

4. Warren W. Wiersbe, *Be Faithful* (Colorado Springs: Chariot Victor Publishing, 1981), p. 106.

5. William Hendricksen, *New Testament Commentary—The Pastoral Epistles* (Grand Rapids: Baker Book House, 1976), p. 365.

6. John MacArthur, Jr., *The MacArthur New Testament Commentary—Titus* (Chicago: Moody Press, 1996), p. 85.

7. H.D.M. Spence and Joseph S. Evell, eds., *The Pulpit Commentary, Volume 21* (Grand Rapids: Wm. B. Eerdmans Publishing Company, 1978), p. 25.

8. Ibid., p. 31.

9. Ibid., p. 36.

10. G. Campbell Morgan, *Life Applications from Every Chapter of the Bible* (Grand Rapids: Fleming H. Revell, 1994), p, 209.

11. Sid Buzzell, general editor, *The Leadership Bible* (Grand Rapids: Zondervan Publishing House, 1998), p. 739.

12. William J. Petersen and Randy Petersen, *The One Year Book of Psalms* (Wheaton, IL: Tyndale House Publishers, Inc., 1999).

13. Charles R. Swindoll, *The Tale of the Tardy Oxcart* (Nashville: Word Publishing, 1998), p. 613.

Chapter 14—Wisdom—An Essential for Godly Living

1. Charles R. Swindoll, *The Tale of the Tardy Oxcart*, quoting from his book *The Strong Family* (Nashville: Word Publishing, 1998), p. 613.

Chapter 15—A Woman's High Calling to Purity

1. D. Edmond Hiebert, *Everyman's Bible Commentary—Titus and Philemon* (Chicago: Moody Press, 1957), p. 50.

2. John MacArthur, Jr., *The MacArthur New Testament Commentary—Titus* (Chicago: Moody Press, 1996), p. 85.

3. William Barclay, *The Letters of James and Peter,* rev. ed. (Philadelphia: The Westminster Press, 1976), p. 94.

4. Bruce B. Barton, David R. Veerman, and Neil Wilson, *Life Application Bible Commentary—1 Timothy, 2 Timothy, Titus* (Wheaton, IL: Tyndale House Publishers, Inc., 1993), p. 270.

5. Both quotes from Michael Kendrick and Daryl Lucas, *365 Life Lessons from Bible People* (Wheaton, IL: Tyndale House Publishers, Inc., 1996), Reading #35.

6. Herbert Lockyer, *The Women of the Bible* (Grand Rapids: Zondervan Publishing House, 1975), p. 45.

7. Kendrick and Lucas, *365 Life Lessons from Bible People*, Reading #127.

8. Ibid., Reading #43.

9. Some words drawn from William Blake, *King Edward the Third*.

Chapter 16—Purity—An Essential for Godly Living

1. Gene A. Getz, *The Measure of a Woman* (Glendale, CA: Regal–Gospel Light Publishers, 1977), pp. 104- 105.

2. Albert M. Wells, Jr., *Inspiring Quotations—Contemporary & Classical*, quoting William Barclay (Nashville: Thomas Nelson Publishers, 1988), p. 167.

3. D. Edmond Hiebert, *Everyman's Bible Commentary—Titus and Philemon*, quoting H. Harvey (Chicago: Moody Press, 1957), p. 50.

4. Title given to Psalm 101 in *The New Scofield Reference Bible*, Authorized King James Version (New York: Oxford University Press, 1967), p. 648.

5. Gene A. Getz, *The Measure of a Woman*, p. 112.

Chapter 17—A Woman's High Calling to Her Home

1. Curtis Vaughan, general editor, *The New Testament from 26 Translations* (Grand Rapids: Zondervan Publishing House, 1967), p. 1017.

2. Homer A. Kent, Jr., *The Pastoral Epistles* (Chicago: Moody Press, 1977), p. 229.

3. D. Edmond Hiebert, *Everyman's Bible Commentary—Titus and Philemon* (Chicago: Moody Press, 1957), p. 50.

4. Warren W. Wiersbe, *Be Faithful* (Colorado Springs: Chariot Victor Publishing, 1981), p. 105.

5. William Barclay, *The Letters to Timothy, Titus, and Philemon,* rev. ed. (Philadelphia: The Westminster Press, 1976), p. 250.

6. Eleanor L. Doan, *The Speaker's Sourcebook* (Grand Rapids: Zondervan Publishing House, 1977), p. 200.

7. *Life Application Bible,* Index of Personality Profiles (Wheaton, IL: Tyndale House Publishers, Inc., 1988).

8. Shared in Elizabeth George, *Beautiful in God's Eyes,* author unknown (Eugene, OR: Harvest House Publishers, 1998), p. 210.

Chapter 18—Homemaking—An Essential for Godly Living

1. Elizabeth Prentiss, *Stepping Heavenward* (Amityville, NY: Calvary Press, 1973), pp. 68-69.

2. Charles M. Crowe, Benjamin R. DeJong, *Uncle Ben's Quotebook* (Grand Rapids: Baker Book House, 1976), p. 200.

3. John H. Sammis, "Trust and Obey."

4. E. C. McKenzie, *Mac's Giant Book of Quips & Quotes* (Irvine, CA: Harvest House Publishers, 1980), p. 312.

Chapter 19—A Woman's High Calling to Goodness

1. Warren W. Wiersbe, *Be Faithful* (Colorado Springs: Chariot Victor Publishing, 1981), p. 106.

2. Eleanor L. Doan, *The Speaker's Sourcebook* (Grand Rapids, MI: Zondervan Publishing Company, 1977), p. 114.

3. John MacArthur, Jr., *The MacArthur New Testament Commentary—Titus* (Chicago: Moody Press, 1996), p. 87.

4. Marvin R. Vincent, *Word Studies of the New Testament—*Volume 4 (Grand Rapids: Eerdmans Publishing Company, 1973), p. 342.

5. Elizabeth George, *Beautiful in God's Eyes—The Treasures of the Proverbs 31 Woman* (Eugene, OR: Harvest House Publishers, 1998), p. 53.

6. John MacArthur, Jr., *The New Testament Commentary—Titus* p. 87.

7. D. Edmond Hiebert, *Everyman's Bible Commentary—Titus and Philemon* (Chicago: Moody Press, 1957), p. 50.

8. Benjamin R. DeJong, *Uncle Ben's Quotebook*, (Grand Rapids: Baker Book House, 1976), p. 209.

9. Ibid.

10. William Hendricksen, *New Testament Commentary—The Pastoral Epistles* (Grand Rapids: Baker Book House, 1976), p. 365.

Personal Notes

Personal Notes

Personal Notes

Personal Notes

Personal Notes

Personal Notes

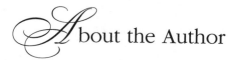# About the Author

Elizabeth George is a bestselling author and speaker whose passion is to teach the Bible in a way that changes women's lives. For information about Elizabeth's books or speaking ministry, to sign up for her mailings, or to share how God has used this book in your life, please write to Elizabeth at:

Elizabeth George
P.O. Box 2879
Belfair, WA 98528

Toll-free phone/fax: 1-800-542-4611
www.elizabethgeorge.com

Books by Elizabeth George

Beautiful in God's Eyes—The Treasures of the Proverbs 31 Woman
God Lights My Path—Meditations
The Lord Is My Shepherd—12 Promises for Every Woman
Loving God with All Your Mind
A Woman After God's Own Heart™
A Woman After God's Own Heart™ Audiobook
A Woman After God's Own Heart™ Growth & Study Guide
A Woman After God's Own Heart™ Prayer Journal
Women Who Loved God—365 Days with the Women of the Bible
A Woman's High Calling—10 Essentials for Godly Living
A Woman's High Calling Growth & Study Guide
A Woman's Walk with God—Growing in the Fruit of the Spirit
A Woman's Walk with God Growth & Study Guide

A Woman After God's Own Heart™ *Bible Study Series*
Walking in God's Promises—The Life of Sarah
Becoming a Woman of Beauty & Strength—Esther
Experiencing God's Peace—Philippians
Pursuing Godliness—1 Timothy
Growing in Wisdom & Faith—James
Putting On a Gentle & Quiet Spirit—1 Peter

Children's Books
God's Wisdom for Little Girls—Virtues & Fun from Proverbs 31